WHITE EAGLE ON
THE GREAT SPIRIT

Also by White Eagle

BEAUTIFUL ROAD HOME

THE BOOK OF STAR LIGHT

THE GENTLE BROTHER

GOLDEN HARVEST

HEAL THYSELF

JESUS TEACHER AND HEALER

THE LIGHT BRINGER

THE LIVING WORD OF ST JOHN

MORNING LIGHT

PRAYER, MINDFULNESS AND INNER CHANGE

THE PATH OF THE SOUL

THE QUIET MIND

SPIRITUAL UNFOLDMENT ONE

SPIRITUAL UNFOLDMENT TWO

SPIRITUAL UNFOLDMENT THREE

SPIRITUAL UNFOLDMENT FOUR

THE SOURCE OF ALL OUR STRENGTH

THE STILL VOICE

SUNRISE

TREASURES OF THE MASTER WITHIN

WALKING WITH THE ANGELS

WHITE EAGLE ON FESTIVALS AND CELEBRATIONS

WISDOM FROM WHITE EAGLE

White Eagle on
THE GREAT SPIRIT

Introduced by Grace Cooke

WHITE EAGLE PUBLISHING TRUST

NEW LANDS · LISS · HAMPSHIRE · ENGLAND

This edition first published November 2003
SUN MEN OF THE AMERICAS published in hardback 1975
Paperback edition 1983

© The White Eagle Publishing Trust, 1975, 2003

British Library Cataloguing-in-Publication Data
A catalogue record for this book is available from the British
Library

ISBN 0-85487-150-0

Printed in Great Britain by
Cambridge University Press

CONTENTS

Bibliography

Three books in particular were an intrinsic part of the early research behind this book. None of them is now easily obtainable, but these are the editions which, as far as is known, were in print at the time of going to press.

THE GOSPEL OF THE REDMAN, by Ernest Thompson Seton. Naturegraph Publishers, ISBN 0839535740.

HE WALKED THE AMERICAS, by L. Taylor Hansen. Guest Cottage, Inc., 1963, ISBN 0910122199.

TOUCH THE EARTH: A SELF-PORTRAIT OF INDIAN EXISTENCE, edited by T. C. McLuhan. Abacus, 1988, ISBN 0349122911.

Also recommended alongside the present volume is WHITE EAGLE ON FESTIVALS AND CELEBRATIONS. White Eagle Publishing Trust, Liss, Hampshire, 2003, ISBN 0854871497.

PUBLISHER'S PREFACE

This book began as quite a personal project by Grace Cooke to document, through the voice of her spirit guide, White Eagle, the special contribution the indigenous American races (across both continents) in earlier times could make to our understanding of how to live today. The project also included research to authenticate the main arguments of the book, both through snippets of archaeological information and through extensive quotation of some of major writings about the 'American Indian' available in her day: classics like THE GOSPEL OF THE REDMAN by Ernest Thompson Seton and HE WALKED THE AMERICAS by L. Taylor Hansen, as well as more contemporary sourcebooks like TOUCH THE EARTH, compiled by T. C. McLuhan. This material was published as Grace Cooke's final book, SUN-MEN OF THE AMERICAS, in 1975, and as such it proved popular enough to go through five printings.

In 2003, there is a rather different need for the material. Much of our understanding of the American peoples has become commonplace, and there is very little need to amplify much of what White Eagle says from elsedwhere, since the experience from which he writes self-evident. There are other parts of the book where what White Eagle says has to be taken more on trust; these are also some of the most interesting pages in the book and may spark further investigation. White Eagle speaks, after all, from his own earthly experience, at least for those who accept the principle of communication from spirit.

The other reason for the different presentation that the book now has is explained by Jenny Dent's introduction. Where once it seemed important to stress the 'Americas' side of the title, the book, now separated from the supporting documentation that interspersed White Eagle's own comment, seems much more to be about ancient brotherhoods and how unreliable the term 'primitive' can be when we talk about primitive peoples. It is a book about humanity's relationship to God, hence the new title.

The very phrase 'the Great Spirit' requires a moment of comment here. Ninety per cent of the time, and in every context in which he was speaking, White Eagle seemed to prefer the phrase 'Great White Spirit'. We are not anxious to play into racial stereotyping, however ridiculous it would be to think of 'white' in this phrase in this way. More curiously, however, 'Great Spirit' is common in North American 'Indian' writings in English, where 'Great White Spirit' is not. White Eagle undoubtedly had a reason for using the phrase, but it seems better to us to note this here than to use the phrase continuously throughout the book.

Another word that needs explanation is 'Indian'. Although the word derives from a misunderstanding by early white colonists that today is somewhat laughable, none of the other words and phrases is entirely watertight either. 'Indigenous American' is probably the best we have but it is a bit of a mouthful and it sounds rather over-contemporary, whereas a great deal of what White Eagle is telling us relates to peoples from history and prehistory who stretched from the Andes, through Central America, right up into present-day Canada and into the Arctic. With all its limitations, the term 'Indian' is useful precisely because it forces us to ask each time what White Eagle means, and to relate what he says to its correct epoch too.

This book is intended to be fully inclusive of gender as well as race—and species. The word 'Brotherhood' (and its derivatives) may seem to go against this. However, the problem is a similar one: define the meaning more closely, and it quickly narrows to exclude other streams of life White Eagle normally wants to include: the creatures, the earth itself, etheric and angelic life, and the continuing life of souls who have passed beyond earth life. What he means by it is indicated by the very first words ascribed to him in the book: 'Brethren of the spirit— for we are all of the same spirit, and therefore brethren....'

These words, along with a number of other passages in the book, have been added for the present title. The three books by other authors mentioned have been largely edited out of the present text (though they are still warmly recommended). What today's reader has in return is more of White Eagle— short, amplifying passages interpolated here and there, the addition of which may go unnoticed even when they make quite an important point. All of Grace Cooke's writing from the earlier volume is retained.

In the text, Grace Cooke's writing is in the smaller type of these three introductions; White Eagle's words are in larger type. Biblical quotation is in italics.

At the same moment as WHITE EAGLE ON THE GREAT SPIRIT is published, comes WHITE EAGLE ON FESTIVALS AND CELEBRATIONS, a book which is its natural companion in subject matter. The reader may like to study that volume after this one.

A PERSONAL NOTE
Jenny Dent

I was privileged to be working with my grandmother, Grace Cooke (or Minesta, to give her the name White Eagle often gave her) at the time she was preparing the manuscript for the original version of this book. My first task had been to research and prepare written scripts of all White Eagle's words about the American people. I then sorted all this material into themes to form the rough outline of possible chapters for the book. As I did this, I became more and more aware of the greater purpose of the book, for the underlying thread throughout all the scripts was of the great brotherhood of all time, and is not limited to one continent alone. What was emerging was a blueprint for a way of life lived in accordance with the divine laws of life (which White Eagle speaks of throughout all his teaching). This blueprint is as relevant now, in the twenty-first century, as it was when White Eagle was giving this teaching through my grandmother, and in the time of the civilizations in the Americas of which he speaks.

In the first two chapters of the book, now entitled 'The Coming of the Sun-Beings' and 'The Brotherhood', Minesta quotes White Eagle's own words about the teachers who came to earth long ago (in different parts of the world) to help humanity learn how to live in accordance with the divine laws.

He tells of the mystery schools which were established and how these were where souls were trained who would to take these truths out into the world for ordinary people to comprehend as they became ready. If one studies the myths and stories surrounding the founding of all our present-day world religions, it becomes clear that the original founders were trained in mystery schools of one sort or another. It is for instance well-known in esoteric circles that Jesus had his early training in the Essene Brotherhood. Perhaps less well known is the probability that Muhammad was trained in the mystery schools of Arabia before the suras of the Koran were revealed. Gautama Siddhartha's journey to 'Buddhahood' and enlightenment reveals a different but equally mystical training and his resulting teaching about the four noble truths and eightfold path is typical mystery-school knowledge.

I should like to share now a personal experience from working with Minesta as she was writing these two opening chapters of the book. Although I had been brought up with knowledge of White Eagle's work and teaching, I had no real experience of 'the Brotherhood' as he here describes it, 'the Brotherhood of the Cross of Light within the Circle of Light'. I had heard of illumined Beings and even heard the words 'Sun-Men' or 'Sun-Being', but had no personal knowledge of them. On one particular day, when I went into Minesta's sunlit study where she worked, all was the same as it was each morning I arrived. At least, all was the same in one way—she was sitting at her desk writing, with books open before her. However, in another way there was something quite different. There was a subtle energy in the atmosphere—an energy of increased light and expectation. It touched me immediately. I had no idea at that time what it meant.

Minesta told me to sit down and take up my shorthand notebook, as she wanted to talk to me about 'the Brotherhood of Light'. As she spoke and I started to write, an incredible light began to flood into the already sunlit little room. The physical sun took on a new dimension and became so bright and strong, yet not the sort of light that would burn the physical body. It was a very nurturing, warm and wonderful light. It was hard to keep writing as I was so bathed in this light, but there was an amazing power that kept me going with the writing, rather similar to the power that enfolded us when I was on the pilgrimage with Minesta to the ancient centres in Britain, which led to her writing THE LIGHT IN BRITAIN in 1971. After a little, I became aware of actual forms within the light, and I saw these beings that she then described as the 'Sun Men', the great teachers who had come to earth so long ago to help struggling humanity learn the true way of living in the heaviness of material life. Within their radiance I felt there was all knowledge, and yet these beings were not intellectual. They were strong yet simple—all the qualities we associate these days with Masters or with the great teachers such as Jesus, Buddha, Ramakrishna, St Francis—the ones we revere in the traditions of every religion. The other thing that struck me was the incredible love they brought with them. It was a love that is quite universal, without any barriers or restrictions. It was a love that was without judgment and one that I knew would never say 'This religion is the right way', 'This culture is the right culture', or anything like that. It was so wonderful and inspiring, and I know it is the energy which is behind all the spiritual awakening that is taking place now as humanity goes forward into the new era—the twenty-first century, which leads to a new golden age. These great beings, the Sun-beings, or as White Eagle latterly refers to them, the great Star Brothers and Sisters—these beings lead human kind forward now into a new phase of brotherhood.

AN INTRODUCTION TO THE NATIVE AMERICANS
Jean LeFevre, Mother of the
White Eagle work in the Americas

As a Peace Elder in the Native American Tradition, it gives me great pleasure to write a few word of Introduction to a book that I originally knew as SUN-MEN OF THE AMERICAS.

My first exposure to the Native American tradition, on its home ground, was early in 1975, when I began to study with Grandmother Twylah Nitsch. Twylah is one of the great teachers; she is a Medicine Person and Clan Mother of the Wolf Medicine Lodge of the Seneca. There was much to learn— and unlearn! I knew that teepees were probably out and that scalping was never indigenous to the Indians (it was a little habit they picked up from the European Bounty Hunters). They appear to have been very gentle people in the early times of their little-known history.

Quite a group of us gathered on that first evening—and

Twylah explained that they began their meetings with the Seneca Power Prayer. This idea did not come as too much of a shock—everyone seemed to be demanding more Power. Why should they be any different? Let the words speak for themselves.

O Great and Eternal Spirit, your love and inspiration I seek.
Every day, every hour, I breathe in your life-giving power:
Power to love, power to care; Power to heal, power to share;
Power to protect, with deeds so pure; power to think with power to endure;
Power to help, wherever there's strife; power to forgive—and to thank you for this life.

This was a wonderful introduction to an ancient belief system; one that was based on twelve Commandments, not ten. These rules may be found in a book called THE GOSPEL OF THE REDMAN by Ernest Thompson Seton.

By the time I met Twylah I had already been involved with the White Eagle Lodge for fifteen years, long enough to be reasonably familiar with the teachings and to have come to know our founders, Grace and Ivan Cooke, quite well. The accuracy of White Eagle's teachings, as brought through by Mrs Cooke, is amazing. The contact healing I experienced was the same—though how one feels may well vary from person to person. Twylah became a member, so I think we can say that she also accepted the authenticity of what White Eagle had to say.

Although my training has been specific to the Seneca tradition, I have had sufficient exposure to other Tribes, Nations and Reservations to know that much of the overall tradition has already been lost. Efforts are being made to revive some of these beautiful ancient teachings and ceremonies, but few people are able or willing to do the lengthy training prescribed by the Elders.

Perhaps it is worth mentioning a few examples. To be a Pipe Carrier, one must (according to the historical tradition) work with the Pipe for twenty-five years. There are very strict requirements—if anyone requests help through the use of a Pipe Ceremony, it must be given—regardless of time or personal convenience. A marriage 'under the Pipe' may not be dissolved. A person does not own a Pipe, but is the caretaker of it. The manner in which the Pipe is handled and the procedures are very strict. Such ceremonies may well be preceded by a period of purification in the 'Sweat Lodge'—and it takes eight years to learn to set up a traditional Sweat Lodge. Sadly, there are a number of unqualified people taking advantage of the current interest in the American Indian traditions—and charging high fees in the process. Obviously, people must eat and in this teachers are no exception. However, the authentic ceremonies are given free of charge, although—for safety reasons—there may be certain requirements before access to such ceremonies is given. A donation or gifts are very acceptable.

Originally the typical gift was tobacco. However, most Elders have as much of this as they are likely to use and may well appreciate something more practical. Monetary gifts are usually acceptable, but no fee is charged for the actual ceremony.

Some of the Reservations are a disgrace—as are the slum areas of most major cities of the world. Some of today's American Indians can be lazy and even unpleasant—as applies to every other ethnic group. Equally, many are good, hard-working and kindly people. However, please do not read this book and expect to come to America, visit a Reservation, and find all the White Eagle teachings being practised as a way of life. We cannot even claim to do that here at the American Center of the White Eagle Lodge—though we try!

It is generally accepted that the present American Indians are the remnants of a once-great people, whose religion was a way of life for them. Even today one cannot find a mere word for 'religion' in any of the Native languages. This is reflected at the heart of White Eagle's gentle teachings—we must *live* what we believe.

One may only speak from one's own perception. I find the other Elders to be amazingly accepting of me as a person. I meet all but one of the qualification required to teach Ceremonies, the exception being my inability to teach the ceremonies in a Native Language—though few others meet this requirement! I have a very real and deep respect and appreciation for most of their traditions, but even traditions evolve—or die. This is not said in disrespect to the People, but with regard to White Eagle's teachings on cruelty and especially as it relates to animals. Although a vegetarian way of life was not unusual in times past, it is rare today. On the other hand, there were once certain ceremonies involving animals that would not be acceptable on humanitarian grounds. To the best of my knowledge, most of these have been discontinued. I trust that this is so!

Tribute should be paid to Grace and Ivan Cooke: their incredible contribution—through books, papers and recorded talks—stands on its own merits. There is an essence in these writings that transcends doubt and brings a sense of confirmation and an awareness of one's own inner truth. This is the real test. Truth is a jewel with many facets, but few have all the truth on any subject, and none can claim to know the truth concerning all things. History is no exception. Almost always, it has been written by people who were not there, describing events they did not see, recalling conversations they did not hear—and reaching some very contradictory conclusions.

Grace Cooke has used a combination of her own far memory and the teachings given to her by White Eagle. Her husband, Ivan Cooke, was her friend, colleague and co-worker. He shared her gifts and was able to use his own talents to work with her and to verify the material brought through. They were, and still are, a team.

There is a growing interest in the American Indians, and they are putting aside past events as they move forward to the twenty-first century. May the gentle and wise teachings of White Eagle help us all to do the same.

1
_____

THE COMING
OF THE SUN-BEINGS

I have known White Eagle all my life, or so it seems to me now. In fact he first made himself known to me when I was quite young. I have a vivid memory of seeing, before I fell asleep at night, what I now know to be a circle of Indians standing round my bed. I knew they were my friends, because they were so kind and looked at me with gentle, smiling faces. They wore bright colours, and I felt happy and contented, with nothing to fear, with them around me. Intuitively I knew they belonged to me, that they were my people, my family.

There was one among the group taller and more impressive than the rest, dressed all in white. This stately old Indian chief would take my dreaming self into the land where lived the spirits of the trees, of the air, of the water, a land of sunlight and happiness—and I came to know and love him very well. Later he revealed himself as White Eagle, my spiritual guide and teacher in this life, and told me of the work we had to do together. *

*Much later, when I was in my middle life, I was shown how many thousands of years ago in South America he had been my father Hah-Wah-Tah. In an earlier book, THE ILLUMINED ONES, I have described my life as Hah-Wah-Tah's daughter.

Through him, I became familiar with the wisdom of the Indians; and he awakened memories for me of my life as an American Indian in the distant past. We lived close to the Great Spirit in those Indian days, and even as children we were taught about the laws of God, the Great Spirit, and shown how to live in harmony with them. We understood that we were just a small part of a vast brotherhood which embraced all creatures on earth and in the etheric world, a brotherhood which extended to include other worlds, other planets. How far back this life was I cannot judge, but I feel it was long ago. Yet whenever I touch this level of consciousness, I am in the present as well as the past and the future—it is all one, there is no time.

But in memory I go back once again to the life when I was an Indian girl living with my family near a swift-moving river. It all comes back to me so vividly, I can hear the rush of water and with it an overwhelming feeling of power. I feel so strong as this great power rushes in and through me; I learn of the power of water, its cleansing and healing property.

I remember seeing an injured man carried down to be bathed in the water; I saw the stemming of the flow of blood, the swift healing of the wound, as if by some magical power, as it was immersed in the water. Some thought it was the man's faith which healed him, but I was told by my Indian father that the healing power in the running water performed the miracle. In those days I remember being taught by our Chief, as we sat in a large circle round the altar fire, that there was healing in all the four elements.

We learnt to look up into the sky and trace the movement of the clouds, and see the forms of the spirits of the air. We looked for the pictures which formed in the clouds and learnt lessons from the changing scene. The Chief explained to us how the wise ones could work with the nature spirits and bring rain to the parched earth. In fact we young ones watched our elders do this. We were taught to look at the animals and birds, trees and bushes and flowers, and even the very stones, and see God, the Great Spirit in them. And so we loved them, and would do nothing to harm them.

We were taught that the air and water were as brother and sister to us, because without them life could not continue on the earth; nor could we live without the light and warmth of the Sun; and that the earth was our mother. These elements were part of our very life, part of ourselves. The fruits and berries, and even the roots of certain plants which were used for food, could not grow without the life-giving power of the Sun and the elements; and so we were taught to worship the life-givers—the earth, air, fire and water.

I remember how we used to sit in a circle or a wheel, with the imaginary four arms of a cross; and in the centre of the cross the wood fire burnt very brightly. We learnt that when the flame ignited the wood, the sunlight imprisoned in the wood was released for the many needs of human life. As we sat round the fire in a circle we learnt many of the secrets of nature and of the laws of the Great Spirit, which had been passed down from generation to generation.

White Eagle has shown me that the teaching of the law of life, or the ancient wisdom, which is the foundation of all religion, was brought to human kind in the beginning of the cycle by those whom he calls Sun-gods, or Sun-beings. They came to earth from afar to a land now submerged, bringing their wisdom to a young humanity, pure in spirit. They taught them the Law of God, and a way of life which would lead them through the bondage of physical matter back again to God, as fully God-conscious beings.

From that early civilization, the Motherland, messengers travelled both east and west, to many parts of the world, carrying with them the original teaching and establishing centres of wisdom: 'mystery schools' which, in remote places, behind the scenes of human life, have been the inspiration of all religion. Wherever they went, the messengers taught the people about the divine laws by which life on earth is ordered, and taught them how to live in harmony with these laws in love and brotherhood. Those who settled in America taught the people, in those ages long ago, the same spiritual truths which the old Chief passed on to the listening circle round the fire.

White Eagle says:

'Brethren of the spirit—for we are all of the same spirit, and therefore brethren—we come into this material, this physical condition, with thankfulness and love. We spare no endeavour to expand this communion between the worlds so as to build an etheric bridge for communication from the higher world to reach the earth more readily. We come, and our brethren come under the Divine Law, to help human kind to quicken their spiritual life.

'Let us go back in thought to a life which is very close to us now. Many of you were there with us in this life, and we in those days had not very white complexions. We had paler skins than you think—perhaps we may be permitted to say prettier skins—and fairer skins than many people know today. It takes more than a skin of any colour to radiate purity and beauty. Remember that those people who are called spirit guides, and who make themselves known to you, may be in a Chinese body, or in an Indian body, indeed in an Eastern body of any nation, or in a body of an ancient American known also as an Indian; and some of these people originate from the Plumed Serpent Brotherhood. All these ancient people have a great deal to contribute in this day and age in knowledge, as well as wisdom, to our poor benighted humanity—because so many humans today are what you would call 'out on a limb'. They are very cold and hungry; they have lost their way, because they have allowed intellect and the body together to dominate and obscure the inner voice, the pure essence of divinity.

'You may only be aware of the remnant of some of the ancient races which were once known as the Red Man, in the Canadian Indians, the North American Indians, and some of the South American Indians of modern life. There is within them—how shall I call it?—untouched memory of a culture which is rich in divine law. Divine law brings to humanity a knowledge of its potentiality, of the individuality of the soul, how the individual can work in harmony with the universe and make contact with the other kingdoms of life. He can learn about the angelic kingdom, the nature kingdom with the nature spirits, and the air spirits and the water spirits, and learn what these spirit angels can do for humanity in daily life.'

White Eagle goes on to talk of the 'mystery schools' mentioned earlier.

'The mystery schools established in the beginning have continued throughout the world's history, spreading to one continent after another. Inscriptions still testifying to the existence of these schools can be found on relics of stone, but the modern investigator does not yet comprehend their meaning. Nor does the modern mind understand one iota of the power and glory and truth still impregnating these stones, in the very earth itself. As surely as the Sun's rays penetrate the earth and all physical matter, so the light of the ancient wisdom still impregnates the stones and the earth about them.

'In the beginning of human life on earth, a great truth was directed onto the planet. It came in the form of the light ... the light of human hearts. It is indescribable. We cannot tell you what it is, it is for you to become aware of it, to realize it. Having realized it, you will draw your strength, your light, for ever more from its true Source. It is the Sun. It is the spiritual Sun which the ancients worshipped, a worship which earthly people have mistaken for worship of the physical form of the Sun. The Sun-worshippers of past ages were not idolaters, but they knew the spiritual meaning of what was the life-giver of their world.

'We who come from the spirit can assure you that the world and humanity are far, far older than you can conceive. Countless years ago men and women met in open temples to worship the Sun. They were not as you are; they were souls who had come to this planet from another to establish centres of power and light on earth. It is the work of the Brotherhood in spirit today to release this ancient light, still imprisoned both within the earth and within all men and women. When this light, this truth, is released, a life more beautiful than any known on this earth for many thousands of years will come again.

'These people were much stronger and bigger than those of today. If you could see them clairvoyantly, you would be struck by their size and grandeur of form, and by the light which shines from them. These are the ancient Sun-beings or Sun-gods, the original brothers and sisters of the Great White Light, who came to earth to establish the inner light by which the race has lived ever since. Strong and fine physically, they were also strong in spiritual power.'*

All down the ages, the ancient ones have appeared

---

* Once, in deep meditation, I had a vision of these very tall, noble-looking beings standing in a large circle of light in space and encompassing, so it seemed to me, the whole earth. It looked like a circle of fire, a ring of pulsating light and power, and in it I saw both human beings and angels.

to men and women in a form which they could accept, and using the language of the day, which the world could understand; they have come to teach the people about God's truth and reveal to them, by degrees, the secrets of earth and heaven. The question arises, why has humanity fallen so far back? It is because in the earliest days human beings lived much more in the spirit than in the body—or shall we say it was a more 'ethereal' life, and they were aware of angels and visitants from other worlds? Since those days humanity has become much more deeply imprisoned in matter. By their own choice, men and women have travelled a hard path. They have had to learn, they have had to pass tests and trials, bringing pain and suffering. But out of these experiences will come something wholly good which will enable all humanity in time to return in full consciousness to the perfect life of its Creator.

2

THE BROTHERHOOD

The belief that the religion and philosophy of the early Americans was brought to them by wise men from afar comes in many stories and legends still remembered by the American Indians. White Eagle himself has told us of the folk tales and myths which remain among the American Indians about the coming of the 'feathered Gods', wonderful beings who came from across the sea bringing light and salvation. Many are the accounts of a sacred one, or prophet, who came to the people from afar off. the description of this personality varies little. I should like to quote a story, reproduced in L. Taylor Hansen's HE WALKED THE AMERICAS, from an American Indian text known as 'The Legend of the Sacred City', which is by an old and revered Indian.

'I came to take you back to the ancients and to the times of our people's greatness. I thought to take the legends with me even into the Land of Shadows, but the young man who came so far to seek me reasoned well before the fire. He said I had no right to silence, for the stories belonged to all our people so long as one Redman walked the earth. They must go on past this generation and to that unborn soul who might be listening and wishing to hark back to the ancients.

'Therefore tonight I am here to take you walking back

through the dawn-star cycles to a time long distant when the land was not as you see it. Past the memories of our grandfather's grandfathers I take you with me to the days of the Healer, and the times of our people's greatness…. Coming north from our Capital City, where the Mississippi meets the Missouri, in the long-boats of the traders, the Prophet made his journey towards the city we called Sacred…. This city was called Sacred because it was in the centre of the Cross of Waters from whence ran the rivers to the Four Oceans. Fast to the sunrise ran the waters, and northwards to the Sea of Dancing Lights; to the west beyond the Great Divide the waters ran to the Sea of the Sunset, while the Missouri and Mississippi ran to the Southern Sea, the Sea of the Karibs.

'To this, the city of the Great Cross of Waters, up the river called the Father of Waters, one golden morning came the Healer. The dawn cascaded down upon him as he left the ships of the merchants, painting his hair and beard with beauty and lighting up his lofty features.

'The streets were petalled with flowers before him as he walked towards the Temple. Greatly beloved now was the Pale-God, known as the Lord of Wind and Water. His every move bespoke his kindness, his very touch revealed his divinity and before him bowed down all people.

'Through rows of temple worshippers he moved in quiet solemnity, holding up his hand in blessing, that hand with the strange palm marking, for through it was engraved the cross which he had taken as his symbol.

'There at the temple he abode among us, though he often rode away with the merchants or more often walked to distant villages, holding in his hand his great staff, and stopping to speak with all, from the aged to the children.'

Many of the legends about the prophetic visitor refer to the dawn star: they tell us that the sainted one taught the people to look to the dawn star for guidance and direction in their lives; that he concentrated on Venus, the dawn star, as a focal point for his aspiration and prayers, and that originally he had come to the earth from Venus. White Eagle too has often referred to the Brotherhood on Venus, and told us that he has 'seen the Sun rise' on Venus.

White Eagle once said of this legendary sainted one:

'The story is that he came mysteriously to the Indian peoples and taught them about the wonderful life beyond the Sun; taught them the lessons of peace, brotherhood and goodwill, and all the beautiful truths which Jesus the Christ also taught his disciples. At the appointed time, the Indians saw him depart. He is supposed to have entered his canoe and sailed away down the river to the west, right into the Sun. His symbol was that of the all-seeing eye. It was believed by the Indians that their saviour was always with them and was watching over them. In a sense his was a magical, a spiritual eye, all-seeing, all-loving, and they knew that his eye was upon them and so all was well.'

From his own memory and vision of the past, White Eagle, goes on to say elsewhere:

'Try to forget all you have read and heard about savage Indians living in wigwams. Not all Indians were nomadic. The Indians of whom we speak had beautiful buildings, beautiful homes. In spite of all the misrepresentations, our ancient Indian Brethren were simple at heart—so simple and loving and gentle. They were people of character and strength of purpose, possessing great courage and endurance. There were many tribes, they spoke many languages and lived at many different levels of development, but one factor all had in common, and this was a deep sense of honour and morality, of goodness. The Indian culture goes back far beyond any known historical or archaeological records of its civilization.

'It is very little understood by the present-day scholar; and it cannot easily be interpreted, because humanity has not developed that spiritual quality which will enable people to read the truth found on the stone tablets and remnants of earlier civilizations buried in the distant forests, not only in South America and Mexico, but in North America too. The civilization of the Indian was one of the most beautiful and ancient civilizations there has ever been on earth.'

What White Eagle calls the Sun-beings or God-beings, those who brought the ancient wisdom to humanity, were messengers from that great Brotherhood of the Cross of Light within the Circle of Light, the Great White Brotherhood, which since the beginning of life on earth has had human kind in its care.

Some of the messengers settled in the Andes and established a centre of the Brotherhood there. White Eagle himself has spoken of his memories of a group of brothers in the Andes who wore white robes ornamented with gold, and plumed headdresses.*

Through the ages the ancient Brotherhood has worked to help men and women in their spiritual evolution and search for truth. Some of its number work in the invisible world, and others periodically take on a physical body to enable them to do a specific piece of work on earth. This, White Eagle has done many times. Two such lives are described in my book, THE ILLUMINED ONES: one when he was Hah-Wah-Tah in America, and the other as the priest Is-Ra in ancient Egypt. White Eagle tells us:

'When we were wearing the attire of the North American Indian, with the power of the Great Spirit we were able to accomplish an important piece of work. We don't speak with the object of drawing attention to a particular personality, but we come back to earth with this personality because our work is closely connected with the American Indian life and the work of the Brotherhood that was begun and established during the prehistoric period. Its symbol was the Cross of Light within the Circle of Light, and it was known as the Brotherhood of the Light, the White Brotherhood, or sometimes as the Star Brotherhood.'

*For Grace Cooke's own memories of a life when White Eagle (known then as Hah-Wah-Tah) was an initiate of this Brotherhood, see the footnote on page 19.

My own first knowledge of the Brotherhood in my present life came many years ago, when I was told by White Eagle that I was linked with an ancient brotherhood; he told me to remember this always and to seek 'the cave of the Brotherhood of the Cross within the Circle'. As my psychic powers developed, I had many out-of-the-body experiences, and I remember on one occasion being taken in meditation to a beautiful place, I do not know exactly where, and finding myself with my guide at the entrance to a cave from which a bright light issued. I was taken into this cave and felt at once the spiritual power which was in the light. An assembly of people robed in simple white habits, with wide sleeves covering folded arms, stood round the cave. They created a great circle of white light, and from north to south and east to west of the cave was drawn also an immense cross of light. I could see that a silent ceremony was taking place, and I was enfolded in a feeling of pure love and power. Illumination is the word to describe what I experienced; I knew that within this wonderful circle of light and love no harm could ever touch me; I felt tremendously strong, and yet so small and humble within its power.

There next came a feeling of absorption, as though I was being absorbed into the light, but instead of losing myself I found I became much bigger and greater than my little self— I became part of the entire company. I was at one with this infinite and eternal circle of light, and the words rang in my cars, repeated again and again in melodious chant, 'There is no death, there is no death, there is no death.' I knew deep in my soul that there was indeed no death. We live forever in the beautiful garden of spirit, and while still retaining our individuality we shall become at one with all life. We shall become as one with the flowers, the trees, the running water, the birds, the animals, the mountains and the valleys. We shall return to the knowledge of the Garden of Eden, the beginning and the end, the complete circle of the Great White Light.

The powerful chanting went on and on, working up to a crescendo of power and ecstasy. I realized I was taking part in a very ancient native American ritual. I have no words to describe adequately the unbounded joy and happiness I felt in this circle of light. How long I held the contact, I have no idea; time was nonexistent. I just *was*, in this glory, this perfect peace and complete happiness; I was united in spirit with all my loved ones. I retained my own individuality but was part of and absorbed by the circle of light, the eternal life.

Thinking about this meditation later, I remembered White Eagle's words of many years before when he had said, 'Look to the Brotherhood from the cave of the Cross of Light within the Circle of Light.' So this is what he meant by the 'cave' or meeting-place (I think the term cave is symbolic of its being within the inner or soul world) where the ancient Brotherhood assemble to send forth the power of light and love to human beings and all creation.

Many years ago I was given a portrait of White Eagle painted under inspiration by R. Vicaji. One of the first features that struck me about this picture was the symbol of the cross within the circle on the left of the headband. This, together with his constant references to the Brotherhood, has convinced me of White Eagle's priesthood in the Brotherhood of the Cross of Light within the Circle of Light.

White Eagle told us something of the inner work of the Brotherhood when he said:

'These brethren who dwell in the mountaintops (which can mean an elevated state of consciousness), who gather together in small groups or lodges in remote places, are working unceasingly for the spiritual unfoldment and advancement of humanity. They have reached a level of spirituality which has brought them into close communion with the Eternal Spirit. They do not live to themselves, however remote their abode, for they are so attuned to the Infinite that their consciousness embraces all life. They can still take on a physical form, for they have passed through and mastered all degrees and grades of human life. They comprehend the slightest, the most simple need of any human being. They are all love and understanding. They do not coerce; they allow their younger brethren absolute freedom. Their work consists of worshipping God their Creator and through that worship they radiate light and love. The elder brethren labour ceaselessly for you and for all, but people do not recognize their benign influence.

'From time to time in the history of humanity, teachers have come to the earth with a new "religion", as it is called. In reality there are no new religions, but only teachers such as the saints and the sages of all time who come to restate spiritual truth. All down the ages these ancient ones have appeared to human kind in a form which they could accept. They have used the language of the day, which the people at that time could understand.

These ancient ones were known by the native American race as the 'Plumed Serpents'. They were so called because through their spiritual greatness they appeared to have a crown of light around their heads which looked like a crown of soft feathers. But it was, of course, just the divine fire, the illumination around the dome or the temple, the higher centres, which caused them to appear to be wearing crowns of white, luminous feathers. They were known as Plumed Serpents or sometimes Feathered Serpents. They came to the priests in the temples and imparted to them the will of God—conveyed to them the will of the Almighty Spirit.

'The names of these ancient ones differed from age to age but always they have come, bringing the light to human kind. They came as saviours. They came to the people in exactly the same way as did Jesus, himself a messenger, a saviour. It was said in ancient days that these souls came from the Sun, or Venus, that they were Sun-gods. These Sun-gods were similar to the one you now worship as Christ, and who of course is Christ the Lord. You think of Christ who illumined Jesus as 'the only-begotten Son of the Father'. This is true. Christ is truly the third aspect of the Deity, the only-begotten of the Father–Mother God, but this universal Christ light has had a number of manifestations apart from the one through Jesus; there have been other Christed ones. Christ is everywhere, infinite, eternal; Christ always has been and always will be. Christ has come again and again, and has always brought the same message.

'In days gone by when we ourselves lived in a body of flesh, we were acquainted with such a one. The message was the same, and the messenger appeared miraculously. As has happened since, the Sun-gods were crucified and they rose again, teaching the people about the mysteries of birth, life, crucifixion and resurrection. These Sun-gods have visited Britain too, but none today knows about them. There are still markings on stones all over the world which record their visitation, and which one day will be read and understood by initiates. These things are only for those who have eyes to see and ears to hear.

'There is a world composed of finer ethers which is just within your own "solid" world; it is not the spirit life, as you understand it, to which you go when your body dies, but something closer to earth. Within this finer world these ancient Brethren of the Sun still live and worship in their Sun temples and cities. Why are the Sun people still around the earth? Because they have work to do with the earth and with human kind. Silently, unknown to humanity, this life goes on, and the spiritual light from it is penetrating the earthly darkness. Men and women think that all good comes from themselves, not realizing that they are just instruments of spiritual forces and the spiritual life. However, they have freewill, they have the power of choice, and they can respond to all that is true and lovely and good; or, rejecting these things and following the path of self, find only darkness and confusion. These are the forces playing upon humanity, both negative and positive.

'The ancient brothers and sisters of the Sun still live and worship in their sun temples and cities. They are still around the earth because they have work to do with the earth and with humanity. Silently and unknown, this wonderful life is being lived, and the spiritual forces are penetrating the earthly life. Sometimes they reach the conscience of individual people, and those people are inspired.

'Through the ages, people have gathered in groups to radiate the light. We speak not of recognized churches or religions but of inner brotherhoods to whom the ancient secrets have always been entrusted.

'Many today are beginning to stir under the influence of the power of the spirit. In some cases their minds are being stimulated instead of their hearts. The mind can be a very cruel taskmaster and lead to destruction; this has happened on more than one occasion when there has been desire for mental power and knowledge without a corresponding development of the heart centre within the soul.

'We could take you to a ceremony where the brethren have great knowledge; where there is immense power. Yet you would not be so much impressed with the depth of knowledge displayed, as overcome by the gentle love, simplicity and humility; and you would learn from such an experience that mental development without accompanying love has no power except that of disintegration. Love is the only power which can create and coordinate all forces and use them for the happiness and progress of life on earth and in heaven. This should encourage you to follow the narrow path of brotherly love.'

White Eagle's words show us that the ancient Brotherhood has been concerned throughout the ages with teaching human kind the age-old spiritual truths upon which all life and religion are founded. The Brotherhood which was established in America became the centre from which this teaching was given to the Indians of both North and South America; these people were shown how to live their whole lives in accordance with spiritual truth and the principles of the Brotherhood. Thus was the work of the Brotherhood centred in America in ages long past and the spiritual blessing and heritage the brothers brought to the American Indian people has remained with them. The Brotherhood has now withdrawn much more from the physical plane than in those far-off days, but their guidance and influence remain.

The symbol of the Brotherhood has a beautiful meaning. The cross is the cross of matter to which men and women are bound while in incarnation, but all the while they are enfolded in the love of God, the circle of light and eternity. Thus the cross signifies the sacrifice and suffering or the bondage of the earthly life; the circle, God's eternal and enfolding love.

3

ANCIENT WISDOM: THE RELIGION OF THE INDIAN

We have seen how the teaching of the Brotherhood of the Cross of Light within the Circle of Light was brought to America by teachers from a continent now submerged, and how centres of the Brotherhood were established there and the people taught the divine laws of life. This teaching is known, very simply, as 'the ancient wisdom'. The ancient wisdom contains all that men and women need to know about their Creator, themselves, and the divine laws which govern life; and in one form or another it has been handed down through the ages from generation to generation all over the world. The beliefs and way of life of the American Indians have their origin in this ancient wisdom; and we, in our present civilization, can learn much from the way of life adopted so long ago.

White Eagle tells us:

'Behind all religions through the ages is one truth. This is the ancient wisdom, brought to humanity in the beginning by God-beings, messengers of the Great White Brotherhood. If you study this ancient wisdom, you will recognize how its influence pervades all religions. It comes to light again and yet again in many a re-presentation.

Whatever the forms or the symbols used to set forth truth, when you go back to the foundation you will find there the seeds of ancient belief, the ancient wisdom. As it was in the beginning, is now and ever shall be. Ancient wisdom sets forth a plan of life which embraces heaven and earth; as it is above, in the heavens, so it manifests below, on the earth. It is the wisdom of the heart; it enshrines knowledge of the divine fires and creative powers with which all are endowed, and of the divine laws which govern all life.

'Fundamental to the ancient wisdom is belief in a supreme being, God, known by many different names in different religions, but as the Great Spirit to the American Indians. The Indian who worshipped the Great Spirit worshipped the whole creation of Almighty Being. The noble Indian gazed at the sky with thankfulness and recognized a Power there. The Indian recognized it in the stars and the planets, in the Sun and the moon, for he or she knew that the planets and stars had a great influence upon the earth and upon his own life. The Indian studied the ways of nature, studied the winds and the rain clouds and the four seasons. Indians recognized that behind all these natural forces there was a directing power with which they could work in harmony, and bring peace and happiness in their own lives by obeying the Great Law as taught by those that came before.

'All the aspirations of the American Indian people went out to this Great Spirit, which they recognized in all its manifestations in life; in the growing corn, in the falling rain—so vitally important to them; in the warm sunshine, in the trees and the flowers. In all the natural life of their world, they recognized the giver of life, the provider of food. The Great Spirit was everywhere for them.'

But White Eagle has taught me that in the ancient wisdom the eternal Spirit is both Father and Mother: the Father, the divine energy; and the Mother, the enfolding love. This is one of the indications he has given of how such a belief felt to him and to his people:

'In ancient times, we learnt to worship not Him but They, the two. We worshipped the Mother God, and we looked to the great Motherhood of all life with adoration, respect and love. To us the Mother promised life. She was the receptacle of the seed of life; the Mother could not produce life without the Father God, but the Father God could produce nothing without the Mother. Therefore, we were taught by our great Teachers of the Spirit to love both Mother and Father. We commend this thought to you all.

'The child of earth looks to its mother for certain qualities, certain gifts. It looks to its father for other qualities. It loves both parents and has confidence in them, knowing that they will not fail it. You also, child of the Father–Mother God, instinctively, intuitively look to a power beyond your own. Thus, in the dawn of life, souls were taught to worship the Mother as well as the Father God. They adored and worshipped the Mother God, the Great Mother, because the mother was the giver and preserver of life, and provided for the continuation of life. A mother has an antidote for her child's suffering; a mother guides wisely the child's first tottering steps; the Great Mother was therefore the adored one. To our people she was the loving, tender mother who was the soul of life and all sustenance.

'In those days, we recognized the Creator as a Mother because we saw the human mother producing her young, and saw nature herself reproducing animal and plant life everywhere. We recognized in the continual sowing and reaping of the harvest, the sequence of the seasons, the birth of our young, an assurance that our own lives would continue after death. Because of this, we became convinced of a Creator above and beyond ourselves, and so we were overjoyed and filled with gratitude for the abundant blessings bestowed on us by some invisible power. We looked up to the heavens, and saw a manifestation of the same invisible power in the stars and the Sun, and we knew that without the Sun, life could not continue because our crops would not grow or ripen. So we worshipped the Mother, and we worshipped the Sun—the Son.

'The Son, born of the Father–Mother God, who descended into earth, was pure light, pure love. That Son is in humanity, the light within every being which is salvation.

'The Christ light, the light of the Son, can make all

things new, just as the light and warmth of the physical Sun brings forth fruit and food on the earth. The spiritual Sun in the heavens is the Son of God, the first-born; and from the Sun, all life on earth comes.

'Our people knew that they were wholly dependent not only upon the physical manifestation of the Sun but also the divine life within it, the divine principle it symbolized. They were taught that they also had within themselves a Sun which radiated from the heart. This light of the Sun within the heart had to become the guiding principle in their lives. If they followed this light, it would lead them always, without fail, to all truth; it would reveal the way to unfold the soul-powers which would bring them into touch with planes of life beyond death.

'They also linked their knowledge of the power of the Sun upon their lives with the influence of heavenly bodies, for there were wise ones among them who were developed mentally and spiritually. These elders studied and meditated upon the movement of the planets and the stars—the heavenly bodies—and as a result they discovered (from the same source as you yourselves are beginning to discover it) the influence of these planets upon human life: an influence quite beyond the comprehension of the brain. They also found that there was something within themselves which was affected by the heavenly bodies. They had what you call a psychic sense or a spiritual awareness. They found that they were able to receive communications from companions who had passed away from physical life, and also teaching belonging to a much higher state.'

The tradition of keeping the light burning 'in honour of the Sun' must surely have been handed down the ages from those far-off days when a light was always kept burning in the temples of the Brotherhood. The ever-burning light symbolizes the spiritual light—the Son of God—within the heart of every man and woman. I quote White Eagle again:

'The symbol of the Sun, which is the circle with the dot in the centre, has been in use throughout ages past. It has been found in remote places all over the earth, plainly indicating to the occultist the widespread practice of Sun worship, which was handed down to humanity from an early continent now submerged. Even in your own bible there are references to Sun worship, but they are not recognized as such.

'There is Sun worship of the outer plane, and there is Sun worship of the inner plane, hidden within the teachings of Christ. How are we to recognize and understand the true Christ–Sun worship, as apart from what some scholars would describe as a "pagan religion" ? The true Christ–Sun worship becomes known to the initiate when that person is vivified by the power of the spirit in his or her own heart centre. An individual may accumulate great knowledge, but it will not get him or her very far until the Sun within becomes ablaze; then he or she knows, without need for proof, that the one, the true and only religion for a child of

God is the worship of the Sun. The basis of all religions has been worship of the One who gives life, the Sun, or the Son whom you have learnt to love and to worship in a human form.

'As we have said, the Sun which the ancients worshipped was not so much the physical Sun as the Spirit which the Sun represented, the golden light, the Giver of Life; and for them, that life took the highest form conceivable by humanity, which was their own form. So this form of the human being, lit by the spirit behind it, became for the ancients their God.

'The inner truth of Sun worship applies to the spirit within men and women, the light within their breasts, waiting to rise as gloriously and powerfully as the Sun in the heavens rises on a summer's day. This is the ultimate fact of life: the growth of the Sun within the breast of each man and woman, until each becomes for him- or herself a Sun-being, a being of God.

'Astrologers represent the Sun by the symbol of the dot within the circle. Freemasons also will recognize this symbol, for real freemasonry too is part of the ancient wisdom, and in common with all religions has its origin in worship of the Sun. The ancients believed such worship was divisible into three parts: first, the rise of the Sun, dawn; next midday, when the Sun was directly overhead; and lastly eventide, when the Sun set. We speak from memory when we say that Sun ritual took place at the rising of the Sun; again at noon; and again when the Sun went to rest.'

The darkness and the light

White Eagle further tells us:

'There are two aspects of life called respectively good and evil. On the one side, the good, are many beings working under the direction of the Christ. On the other are hosts who are called evil, or Angels of Darkness, who although their work is different from the Angels of Light are still working within God's law. If you accept God as infinite you must recognize that the power of the Angels of Darkness and destruction is still within the hand and under the control of this infinite Power. Otherwise there would be absolute chaos; otherwise you could have no faith, no confidence, no trust in that divine love which has been preached to human kind through the schools of mystery teaching, which in their turn have fed the religions throughout the ages. Always, there has been revealed to the true pupil of the Master an infinite love, guiding, protecting, inspiring and bringing good out of apparent chaos.

'We would draw your attention to the importance of balance. These two aspects, light and dark, positive and negative, are working together to bring about balance and equilibrium, which is one of the fundamental laws of life. The ultimate is absolute balance within the microcosm, and within the macrocosm. Thus the two aspects of life, good and evil, seen from the higher state of consciousness, are two forces working together to produce the perfect life, and the power of mastership in the individual life. As well as invisible presences, invisible beings outside him- or herself, there is also that within every man and woman which is both positive and negative, light and dark. What must be remembered is that you hold the balance within your own heart. It is of vital importance that this balance between the positive and negative should be kept.'

Long ago the God-beings taught the Indians about the two opposing forces constantly at work in all life; and this knowledge has found expression right down the ages in myths and legends handed on from generation to generation. Closely linked with this question of good and evil is that of the creative power (which can be used either for good or evil) which lies in everyone: the 'serpent power', as it is known. The symbol of the serpent was often used by the Indians in the ancient wisdom. It stands for knowledge and wisdom, the wisdom which comes to each one with the rising of this spiritual essence within. This serpent power normally rests sleeping in the human being until it has developed moral strength. If the knowledge is stimulated before spiritual and moral balance has been gained, chaos and destruction follow. In more highly-evolved souls, it manifests in the form of spiritual wisdom and spiritual illumination, which brings the man or woman very close to God. In less-evolved souls, it is the great tester, for when a soul in its ignorance uses this power for its own ends it always has to suffer as a result of its ignorance; but through pain the soul learns, and so it moves forward into consciousness of God.

4

THE GREAT COMMUNION

White Eagle once told us:

'In our American Indian life we were accustomed to sitting in circles. We always sat in a circle, and when we had a meal we always communed with the god of fire, with the Sun; the fire burned in our midst in the centre of the circle. It was a symbol of the ever-burning fires of life. It never went out. It may have died down but it always flared up again. When we took food we always cast a piece of our food into the fire. We gave back to the Creator, the Great Spirit, part of the gift which He–She had given to every child.'

The symbol of the circle, and the dot within the circle (the astrological symbol of the Sun) has always had a special significance for the Indian, symbolizing for him the all-enfolding love of the Great Spirit, the eternity of life, and the universal circle of love and brotherhood to which all creation belongs. T. C. McLuhan, in TOUCH THE EARTH, quotes Black Elk, an Indian of the Oglala division of the Teton Dakota, as saying:

'You have noticed that everything an Indian does is in a circle, and that is because the Power of the World always works in circles, and everything tries to be round. In the old days when we were a strong and happy people, all our power came to us from the sacred hoop of the nation and so long as the hoop was unbroken the people flourished. The flowering tree was the living centre of the hoop, and the circle of the four quarters nourished it. The east gave peace and light, the south gave warmth, the west gave rain, and the north with its cold and mighty wind gave strength and endurance. This knowledge came to us from the outer world with our religion. Everything the Power of the World does is done in a circle. The Sky is round and I have heard that the earth is round like a ball and so are all the stars. The Wind, in its greatest power, whirls. Birds make their nests in circles, for theirs is the same religion as ours. The Sun comes forth and goes down again in a circle. The Moon does the same, and both are round.

'Even the seasons form a great circle in their changing, and always come back again to where they were. The life of a man is a circle from childhood to childhood and so it is in everything where power moves. Our teepees were round like the nests of birds and these were always set in a circle, the nation's hoop, a nest of many nests where the Great Spirit meant for us to hatch our children.'

Someone who is lost—say in the Australian bush—will wander endlessly in a circle: a straight line is always found slowly to bend until it rejoins itself; everything resolves itself into a circle. The beginning is the end, the end the beginning. As White Eagle tells us:

'In the beginning was the Word; and that Word was vibration, a mighty sound which vibrated and reverberated in an ever-widening circle. All creation is within that circle. Think of your life as being held in a circle of light in which you are enfolded; and that you are living within that Word, within that circle of light and power and protection.'

And thus every Indian regarded life; he–she saw it as a circle where death, instead of being the end, was the beginning of the new life in the heaven world—before the next spell of life on earth. Thus life continued eternally like a circle or an upward-winding spiral. Even today, knowledge of eternal life, and of reincarnation, persists among the Indians.

White Eagle has often told us that our life and thoughts here on earth will affect and be reflected in the conditions we shall find when we pass into the next world; and also how our thoughts will affect any future life and physical body we have.

'You have freewill insofar as your create your own future. As you think, as you live, as you act today, you are creating your future life, not only in the spirit world without your body, but in your next incarnation, and probably several incarnations beyond that. You can be master of your life, but not immediately: you can control your immediate reactions, your attitude towards life; you have that freewill determination.

He also says, about this life and the next:

'The ancients … were taught, as you are being taught today, that man cannot injure his brother or sister without self-injury, and without affecting the whole structure of spiritual life. Jesus came with the same message: *Thou shalt love the Lord thy God with all thy heart, with all thy soul and with all thy mind; and thy neighbour*—thy brother—*as thyself. Upon these two laws … hang all the law and the prophets.* So simple a law, and yet in modern life so largely disregarded.'

The Indians knew that life continues for ever and ever. They knew that as season follows season, as winter gives way to spring, so, after death (or a period of refreshment in the hereafter), comes renewed life. They knew that the earth life is a school in which, through experiencing joy and sorrow, people eventually learn the wisdom of God.

'But we are impressing upon you that you must expand your consciousness and your comprehension of life beyond the threescore years or a century or a century and a half, whatever it is you are going to live, in this present incarnation. Remember that life always has been, and always will be, and what you are today is the result of what you lived yesterday. You created your own destiny today; therefore that destiny is implanted indelibly upon the white ether.'

The Indian looked forward with thanksgiving to release from the bondage of physical life into the land of the hereafter.

Every Indian had his or her own Death Song and would quietly sing it in preparation for the great transition of death. It was a song of courage and thanksgiving which helped him or her to go forward into his new life with fortitude and equanimity. In the very early days, the physical remains of a family were always buried in a circle, symbolizing the eternity of life and God's love, and the fact that rebirth follows death, just as spring follows winter.

White Eagle tells us:

'Our Indian people were well aware of the hereafter and the etheric world. They certainly didn't need to be convinced by a medium that there was a hereafter. The Indian child was brought up with this knowledge. The Indians had none of the fear of death that the modern world has, and among the American Indians, you will find evidence of communications from superior beings in the world of spirit.

'Our Indian brothers and sisters knew when their time was coming, and bade farewell, happily, serenely, to their friends to be left on the earth plane; then they climbed to the heights, or went to a still pool, and there laid down the body they no longer needed. This way of living, and of 'dying', will come again when men and women have learnt to be more still, to have more faith, and when they have found the wisdom which will come to him when he has learnt to love … to love all life, and above all to love God.'

Indian children were taught from childhood how to listen to the spirit world. In order to hear the voice from the world of spirit, they were taught first to listen to people on the earth plane—to give their whole attention to the one who was speaking to them. They were taught to listen also to sounds of the birds and animals, the song of the wind in the trees, and the song of falling raindrops and the rushing river. White Eagle says:

'This is how the Indians were trained from childhood, and because they were so trained, they were able to hear not only physical sounds, but sounds behind those of earth: the sounds of the unseen world. They could distinguish the voices of their spirit guides and teachers; they could also hear the voices of the nature spirits. It is difficult for you in these noisy cities to hear anything of these, yet you must train yourself to listen.'

Ancient wisdom reveals that one can teach oneself, from birth into the physical life, to remain in constant awareness of the world of light—the heaven world which surrounds and interpenetrates all physical life. The next world—what some people call 'heaven'—is not far away beyond the stars, but here, around us all the time. We cannot see it with our physical eyes, because it is composed of much finer substance vibrating at a different rate from physical matter. We can train ourselves, however, to use our inner senses to contact this other world, and if these inner senses are developed from birth, when the soul is so very close to that world from which it has just come, they become so active that the person can 'tune in' with ease to people and conditions in the next world. The ancient Indians were taught how to develop their inner faculties long before their lower minds or intellects became so strong and full of material facts that all else was denied existence. This same knowledge was passed on, from generation to generation, right down to modern times.

It is clear that the Indians were well aware also of the importance of a pure and healthy way of life, and strict discipline of the body in order to be able to maintain true awareness of the spirit world, and as pure a contact as possible. They were taught that closeness to nature and the natural life promoted closeness to God; and that spiritual communion with the Great Spirit and the life within all creation can be found in the stillness of the innermost heart during deep meditation. Throughout the ages since, the Indian has always retained this close contact with nature.

When our Indian brother or sister was communing with nature, perhaps gazing on a beautiful landscape or seascape, watching the light dancing on the water, listening to the song of the birds, or looking at a perfect sunrise or sunset, his or her spirit was deeply affected, and this created a sense of joy and peace which pervaded his or her daily life. Our Indian brethren lived every day in such close communion with nature that they were able to realize the universality of God far more easily than we can today. In their peaceful, tranquil way of life, they were in continual communication with the inner world of spirit.

They knew how easy it is to become so absorbed with earthly pursuits and cares that the fragile bridge between the two worlds collapses, and that in order to develop their inner faculties and retain the clear vision into the spirit world with which they were born, a period of each day must be devoted to meditation and conscious aspiration to the heaven world.

White Eagle adds to this:

'In days of old, when the Sun was a symbol of worship, men and women believed that the visible Sun was an outward visible manifestation of an inward light and love. They learnt how to free themselves from the imprisonment of the physical body, leaving it at will, while they, the sons and daughters of the light, journeyed forth, rising above the earth and the fogs and mists of the astral plane to function consciously in the heaven world, while still attached by the silver cord to the physical body. You too can learn to do this.

Don't think that because you have no apparent psychic power you must remain stationary. That is a fallacy. Through meditation, through prayer and aspiration, you can rise above this physical plane, in thought, in your higher mental body, and function consciously in the heaven world. You need not die in order to pass through the second death, the laying-aside of the earth personality. You can enter the heaven world in full consciousness, even though living in the body of flesh.

'We advise you to make a habit of daily communion. We have told you this before, and we shall tell you again and again. Reach up, not from the brain, but from the silent sanctuary in your heart. As you turn within, you will find you enter a world which will expand and grow. You will no longer feel that you are enclosed as in a small chamber. It is rather like the old fairy tales of the little girl who dropped into the well and fell deeper and deeper down the shaft. Instead of being drowned, when she reached the bottom of the well she found herself in fairyland—a land of great beauty. She was inside her own soul world.

'This is something like true meditation. If you concentrate on the quiet place within, you will become lost to the outer world. The outer things fade from your consciousness and after delving deeply into your well of truth you will find yourself in a beautiful and spiritual world. You will be able to walk and talk with the inhabitants of that world. Released from earthly bondage, you will know the glory of the spiritual life. When you want to contact the light and the power and the help from those on high, just open your heart in love, to God. Then visualize a radiant Star just above you. As you concentrate on that Star, it will increase in size and become more brilliant as the rays descend from those celestial spheres and pass right through you, recharging you with power and light.'

Our Indian brethren were taught from time immemorial the importance of maintaining their pure contact with those on high. Every student and seeker after spiritual truth and vision needs to set aside a certain period of the day for meditation and contemplation.

The young Indian sought out the highest summit in the surrounding area for his or her meditation. Symbolically this means making a conscious effort to reach the highest possible point of spiritual consciousness, there to commune with the Great Spirit in the inmost being. The young Indian knew that in rising to the heights, to the highest level conceivable, he or she could not be distracted by the material thoughts which inevitably come crowding into the human mind unless it is consciously directed to some particular point of aspiration. The Indian also knew that this aspiration would immediately take him or her right above the astral planes where undesirable influences and entities lurk.

The Indian went practically naked to meet the Great Spirit. Symbolically, this can be interpreted as the soul being stripped of all material concerns and thoughts, stripped of desire for material wealth, and equal in every way with his brother or sister. The meditating Indian stood 'naked, erect, silent and motionless'. He or she was not only silent in body, but silent also in thought, emotions and spirit, listening to the voice of his Creator. His or her soul was like a still pool of pure clear water awaiting the reflection of his Creator upon it. The Indian stood erect and motionless in spirit as well as in body. The spirit in this upright body was a shining sword awaiting the hand of the Master, the Great Spirit, to use the soul in service according to His–Her divine Will. In White Eagle's words:

'Would that men and women would seek the silence more often, as we used to do in past ages. In our Indian days we who had the welfare of the people at heart would climb high into the mountains to meditate at the rising and the setting of the Sun, and we would not leave our post until we had an answer to our prayer. We did not attempt to solve our problems amidst the noise of the camp fire, but repaired to the mountaintop—not only the physical mountain, but the mountain of the higher consciousness.'

The Indian recognized the great power which lay in the silence. He or she knew how to be silent, and how to use the silence—a gift which we today have lost. Our world is noisy and we have forgotten how to listen to the still sounds of nature; we could learn much from the Indian, had we enough humility.

White Eagle, speaking of the nature of true prayer, says:

'Those who are accustomed to meditate will know that at a certain point you can touch the great silence, the centre, the source of all good. As we have already said, the most ancient of symbols is the dot within the circle, the symbol of the Sun (or the Son, the Christ, the Son of God). To pray truly is to touch the timeless eternal centre, and this has a most powerful effect both on yourself and those around you. You have asked for divine love, and it has been given, because you have asked in the right way. First of all, you have to pray rightly; then you have to seek rightly; and then to act rightly, inspired by right thought. In other words, you have to be true, to act from the centre, from the dot within the circle, from the Christ within. And the way to contact this Christ within is to find the great silence at the centre of all life.

'At this stage, brotherhood of the spirit, brotherhood of all life, is realized by men and women. When, in the deep silence, man–woman knows God, he–she knows all. "Know thyself; know God within the silence, and thou shalt know … all; thou shalt know the universe in which thou livest." This is the basic and simple truth inherent in all religion, and in all good, true men and women. When the critical earthly mind and analytical faculty get to work, that sweet, pure truth becomes covered up; and the brain, instead of being the servant, becomes the counsellor, the dictator. The earthly mind has a capacity for concealing the real; therefore you have to become very strong in your conviction and in your devotion to God. Truth can never be destroyed, but it can be so deeply buried that for a time it is lost to the sight of those active only on the worldly level of consciousness.'

We have seen how the ancient Indians were taught that all forms of life are created by the Great Spirit and the Earthly

Mother, and that all human kind and all the creatures of the earth, air and water belong to one vast family. All life is contained within the circle of the Great Spirit's care and protection.

Animals were never killed indiscriminately; if it was necessary to kill, for food, this was always done with reverence and thankfulness for the life given. The love and care the Indians extended to all animal life was also devoted to the earth itself and all plant life—for, as we have seen, they knew the earth was the Mother of their life and that without the fruits of Mother Earth, they would soon die. In White Eagle's words:

'We would speak to you about the great Communion which you will celebrate when you become aware that you are part of the whole glorious life of God, the Heavenly Father and the Earthly Mother. Brotherhoods of all time have performed the same ritual and worship of the Divine Fire of life, the Source of life, and the Great Mother. You too should meditate on Mother Earth, who sustains you with food for your physical body and your soul: the great Mother Earth who brings forth the beauties of nature and enfolds all her children to her heart. Try to open your consciousness, your soul, to this quiet, gentle mother love. It will comfort you in times of stress. It will heal you in times of pain. Remember always the gifts which have been prepared by God for your healing, your peace, your happiness. They are incomparable with the things which men and women seek on the earth plane. Material possessions, enjoyments of the flesh, all these things crumble and die and can be swept away in a moment, but that deep rich happiness and peace which comes from communion with God can never be taken from you, either on earth or in the world of Light.

'When you are given the symbol of the bread, try to think of its true meaning. Not only the cosmic bread, which you all need constantly, but everything you eat is given to you by God and comes from the Cosmos. So every meal and every crumb of bread you eat should be communion with God. Do you know in our Indian life we would never eat without first giving thanks and blessing the food?* And as we ate we accepted the food as God's gift to us. We hear your thought, "What about eating meat?". We answer, when forced to eat flesh, accept it with a humble and thankful heart, with gratitude to the little brother animal or sister fish who has supplied that food. But it is better still for men and women in their evolved state to eat only the fruits and seeds of the earth, for these are all much better for the purified physical body. The time is coming when conditions will be such on the earth that men and women will be fed entirely by the purest food supplied by the great Mother Earth.

'All food accepted and eaten with thankfulness is a true act of communion. Even the fresh spring water, and the juice of the grapes or the fruits of the earth made into wine, that too is the gift of the Creator.'

*See Chapter 5

To sum up, again in White Eagle's words:

'The Indians had learned through observation of nature, and living in natural conditions, some of the secrets of the invisible power which they called the Great Spirit, by whose laws they endeavoured to live. They believed that the Great Spirit is in all nature, in all creation, in all people.

'As the Indian gazed into the sky he or she saw countless stars, and in this object lesson realized he or she was a part of a vast universe; part of invisible, eternal and infinite life; and realized that life goes on and on. The Indian knew that through right attitude and behaviour his or her own life would travel steadily towards the golden world above.'

5

THE INDIAN AND NATURE

We have seen how the American Indian understood the Great Spirit to be a Being not far removed from earthly life, but in fact present in all creation. The Indian recognized God in the mountains and the valleys, in the Sun and the stars, in the rivers and the lakes, in the forests and the flowers and in every living creature. To the Indian the beauties of nature were a living expression of the love of the Great Spirit and His–Her eternal Presence, and thus a vital part of everyday life.

White Eagle says:

'You are so accustomed to the beauty of nature that you tend to take it for granted. Sometimes your attention may be arrested by a flower, a landscape or a seascape, or even by the glory of the sky at night filled with myriad stars. Then you may say, "Oh, the beauty is breathtaking." Or you gaze upon a rose, perfect in colouring and perfume, and say to yourself, "It is heavenly!"—little realizing the truth of your words; for a perfectly-developed flower is indeed heavenly, inasmuch as it is a manifestation of the life of God, the life of heaven.

'There are some who can see beyond the physical

manifestation; they can use finer senses than the physical; they are able to use their feeling, and as they stand lost in wonder before some scene of natural beauty, by power of imagination they can feel the presence of God beyond the physical form. This was true of our Indian brethren. They dwelt always in a natural environment and were so in love with nature—with trees and water and starry skies—that they participated in the life of the invisible, natural worlds. They were able to see the nature spirits and elementals, and they believed in spirit life.

'The teachers of our own Indian race taught the young through their love of nature, their love of the skies, the winds, and the earth, the flowers, and the birds. When we were incarnate in an Indian body, our children would be brought to us to be named. If it was a male child, we would look into the sky; and the first thing we saw in the sky would give us the name for our child. Perhaps it would be a bird, or a cloud, sometimes a star of shining silver, or brilliant blue. So we would name our child Blue Star, or Silver Star, or Silver Cloud. But if it was a female child we would look upon Mother Earth; we would look at the flowers, at all that grew upon the earth, and the little brooks that ran through the land. We would look down to Mother Earth for the name of our daughter, and we would look up to the skies for our son. You see we were imbued with the importance of nature in our lives. Nature was our teacher; beyond nature we found the soul, the higher ether; and beyond that we found the Great White Light, which was the Spirit of our Father–Mother God, the Great Spirit.'

He says elsewhere that running through all nature, and in harmony with the Sun-beings, is the same language.

'If you would train yourself to understand, go into the country, lean with our back against a tree trunk so that you may hear the language of the trees. Listen to the song of the wind as it rustles the leaves. It has a message for you in the language of the Gods, the language of the old Indian, the old Maya, of the old, old races.

'Learn the secrets of the language of the Gods. Listen to the running water, the bubbling, dashing, purifying, cleansing water, which is purity, filling you with the life-force of God—again the language of God speaking to you. And the flowers, the tiny flowers—the language of God teaching the lesson of humility. See how the little daisy grows; it does not say, "I am fine; I am a beautiful daisy". It grows quietly, whispering to you its message, in the language of the Gods.'

In SPIRITUAL UNFOLDMENT II, White Eagle says:

'The elementals and fairy creatures which abound in the life of nature are all intimately concerned with humanity's spiritual evolution, with its joys and with appreciation of nature's beauty. It is therefore necessary for the soul advancing on the spiritual path to become aware of these invisible helpers at some stage of its journey.

'Many concentrate their whole attention on human survival, while their consciousness of the little people, the nature spirits, is quite closed. They are totally unaware of these little brothers and sisters, and their knowledge of the world of spirit is thus limited. At a certain point on the path of unfoldment the soul's vision clears and it becomes conscious of its little companions all around.

'We have already spoken about the four elements, and have explained that interpenetrating the four physical elements is a finer ether not perceptible by physical sense but which can be registered by that human sixth sense, the intuition or the "psychic" sense. It is from the substance of this finer ether within the four elements that fairy people are created, and thus these etheric creatures can be registered by the human etheric vision. For instance, this finer ether, which is interpenetrating the earth and the earth-ether, is the substance from which the little people called gnomes, the spirits of the earth, are created.

'There is a water-ether, a substance behind and within physical water substance, and from that water-ether are created those spirits called undines or water spirits. So also with the fire and the air. From the element of fire, the fire-ether, are created the salamanders, whose work is to bring live fire into manifestation. Within the ether of each element, and created from it, dwell the creatures associated with that element.

'The air is full of the creatures associated with the air element and created of the air-ether, some quite small, some larger than men and women. Especially they can be found among mountains. If you go into the high and solitary places far from human contacts, there you will become aware of the presence of the mountain spirits, sylphs or the air spirits. They are powerful and mysterious, and do not always welcome the intrusion of people. As an instance we would cite the mysterious difficulties sometimes experienced by mountaineers. The spirits of the air do not suffer human physical intrusion beyond a certain point.

'Wonderful spirit beings such as these inhabit the finer ethers. In your meditations you can, if you work hard, penetrate these heights or these inner worlds. That is what you are endeavouring to do; not in your physical but in your astral body you can visit the settlements of the fairy people; you can see their fairy palaces within the earth, inside the mountains.

'All these finer states of life interpenetrate your physical life. You see matter as a solid mass and find it difficult to believe there can be another life within this apparent solidity. You forget that matter is really only loosely knit and can be interpenetrated by other forms of matter, vibrating at different rates.'

On another occasion White Eagle said:

'From babyhood the young Indian was brought up with reverence for Mother Earth and the great company of nature spirits and elementals. A soul returning from the spirit world into a young physical body retains for some years the ability to see clearly into the finer ethers surrounding the physical. For this reason very young children easily see nature spirits and elementals, and it is only the gradual development of the lower mind and the ignorance of surrounding adults that dims this faculty in later years. But the Indians understood and worked with these little people and brought up their children to do the same.

'When you look upon the beautiful spring flowers, the tender early leaves of the trees, the wonderful green of the shooting corn, all manifestations of the beauty of God's spirit, remember that the brown earth does not produce these beauties alone. The brown earth has to be blessed, has to be tended by the creative Spirit. The brown earth is the symbol of the Great Mother, the Mother God, and is the seed-bed for all the gifts to human and animal life and all creation. Mother Earth is the seed-bed, but without the spirit of the Heavenly Father, without that divine Energy and Will nothing could grow; without the command of God to the sunlight and the warmth, to the wind, air and water currents, nothing will grow. The law of God causes the rain to come and bless the earth—although there are times when people get very disgruntled about the rain. Remember that the rain and the air and the sunlight are all part of life.

'We want you to try to become aware of the vast company of angelic and etheric beings who are agents

of God's law. The ancient brethren of the Great White
Light, the brothers–sisters of the Cross of Light within
the Circle of Light, have always known of this grand
company of nature, of the angels directing etheric
workers in the four elements. In time you will have
evidence that the ancient brotherhoods knew how to
call upon the help of the angels of earth, air, fire and
water. Every great being of the elements has in its
charge and service innumerable fairies, water spirits,
air spirits, gnomes, and fire or Sun spirits—all the
elementals attached to the four elements. All work together to serve the Great Mother. The Indian brethren revered Mother Earth, and understood that the
earth is the womb of life.

'The harvest which blesses human kind is the result
of a direct and perfect law operating with perfect precision from the centre of creation. There is no such
thing as chance. Everything works according to law;
and you yourself have within your being a seed holding the promise of a golden harvest, a harvest of the
perfect life, spiritually and physically, a life eventually
made perfect by that law.'

In the far-off days which saw the flowering of the Indian civilizations, Mother Earth was tended with loving care. The wise
Indian understood with his or her heart what present-day ecolo-
gists are only just now discovering with their minds, that everything in the natural world is interdependent. If one thing is
destroyed, another suffers or becomes over-abundant, and the

fine balance of nature is upset. The Indian learnt how to work with nature and to use natural substances to the fullest advantage to enrich the soil and the harvest.

'Ancient wisdom teaches that behind the physical Sun is the spiritual Sun or the white light, and the ancients were taught how to use and direct this white light for the blessing of their life on earth. They were taught how to work with the angels to control the elements. They learned how to make contact mentally and spiritually with the forces of nature, and how to live and work in harmony with them.

'They were taught, for instance, how in the act of breathing in the fresh air they could also establish contact with the angels of light. An angel is a messenger from God; therefore these angelic or nature forces were able to direct rays of light—power, wisdom and love— to those with knowledge, and through certain practices (notably in meditation and in their way of life) these Indians were able to form very true and beautiful links with those natural forces, and even with the great devas themselves.

'As you unfold spiritually, you will be able to see, even as the ancients did, the spirits of the air: the sylphs and tiny fairies. You will see the angels of the water element, and those lesser spirits who work under their command—the water sprites, the undines. You will see the spirits associated with the earth element—the fairies and the gnomes. The ancient peoples were helped by these angelic powers and nature beings to enrich the soil by the power of the spirit. They had the secret of how to work within natural law to maintain the fertility of the soil, and in ceremonies, perambulations and invocations they called down the invisible forces to bless their lives. In these invisible forces they knew there were vast armies of nature spirits whose cooperation they invoked.

'Looking back, my brethren, down our path of life, we have a memory: the picture of an ancient American life: of a time when the brethren were all united in love, when they understood and worshipped the Great Spirit. Because they had touched the centre of life, they comprehended the power in that life and in the light, and they knew that without a supply of the heavenly food Mother Earth would become exhausted. So these ancient Indian brethren used to gather on the plain to invoke the blessing of the Almighty Spirit.

'That same white light can still be called down, gathered in to the earth to give nutriment, not only to help the grain to burst and send forth its shoot; but also to make it grow to perfection. Those of you who have gardens, and who are lovers of nature, will remember what we say that the finest fertilizer you can give to your crops is the white light, the love of God.'

White Eagle tells us in MORNING LIGHT:

'Light exists even in the substance of the earth. Light is the life of God. It brings life to the physical body and all creation. So the object of human life is to discover this secret, to use this secret to become a true instrument of the light, a perfect light of God, a S-U-N of God. Love is the key and the only key—we say it without equivocation—which will unlock the gate to heaven, which will unlock the gate to the temple of the holy mysteries. You may read whole libraries; you may study all kinds of physical science, but you will not find love. There is only the one way to true wisdom, to true comprehension of yourself, of your life and of the whole universe. The sooner your earthly scientists realize this, the quicker will they discover those inner secrets of nature they struggle to learn. Meanwhile the secrets have to be withheld, because humanity must first learn the true meaning and the vital importance of love.'

'The Indians had this secret knowledge of agriculture and how to grow food, and of the potentialities of Mother Earth. They understood the powers of nature. They understood the occult power which permeated the universe, and that it could be used by men and women for the blessing of all. "Well," you will say, "why don't they give it to us now?" For the simple reason that until humanity has evolved beyond greed and selfishness, beyond the state where the one thought is to make everything pay and to get more money, humanity is not ready for the knowledge. Men and women would only destroy themselves if they were given the occult knowledge which the ancient Indian peoples possessed, before they are ready to receive it.'

This great race possessed the purity, beauty and nobility of character essential for such knowledge to be used for the good of the whole community rather than for the greed of a few. To be able to work in harmony with nature rather than against it was not only known to be in accordance with the law of the brotherhood of life, but it was also vitally necessary for survival. In an affluent Western civilization, people do not starve if the harvest fails; but in those days failure of Mother Earth to produce a bountiful harvest was a very serious matter. Thus the knowledge was of vital importance and was used for the good of all, so that the success of the harvest was dependent not on the vicissitudes of the environment but upon these ancient people's ability to control natural forces.

Some remnants of this ancient knowledge have been handed down through the ages to the wise ones of each generation, and even the Indian chiefs of much more recent times retain it to some extent. I remember some years ago meeting Oskenonton, the American Indian who came over to this country to take the part of the medicine man in a presentation of 'Hiawatha' at the Royal Albert Hall in London. We had a brief conversation outside the Green Room, in the course of which he told me that he was going to America the following week because his people needed him to take part in the ceremony of calling down the rain upon their crops, which were in sad need of water. He said that it was part of the ritual of the Indians to get into sympathetic contact with these natural forces, and by a certain occult method they were able to bring rain, or sunshine, and help the crops in Mother Earth to grow in the finest possible way. So this Native American whom I met and had conversation with was able to confirm for me that this was still part of the 'modern' Indian way of life.

White Eagle tells us:

'The initiates had the knowledge and the wisdom to command the forces of the air and the earth, fire (the Sun) and the water. They had the power to control and direct these cosmic forces. We want you to understand that in the most simple way the Brotherhood in the past mastered and directed air currents, the rainfall, and the light and life from the Sun into Mother Earth.

'In years to come your scientists will learn to do this by some machinery on earth, but in time you too will learn to go back to the ancient way of soul and mental control of the forces of the air. We want you all gradually to understand and learn the power of creative thought, God thought; we want you to understand and work in harmony with the natural and spiritual laws which govern all life. We want you to learn to thank God for every manifestation of these laws, even if it sometimes seems dark and difficult. Remember, without the rain you would have no harvest, and would wither and die. You have to learn to understand and accept the natural law as the ancients did, to love and rejoice in the rain as well as the sunshine. This is a secret which is most important for humanity to learn.

'Many people today would say the ancients were superstitious. But they were not superstitious; they had truth which people today have not yet found. Indians in those days were taught consciously to inhale the light and life-force in the air; to meditate on nature, on the beauty of the grass and the corn and the flowers and the trees and all the blessings of nature. And also they were taught that when they went to rest at night their last thoughts should be of God and of the attributes of God; they should open their souls to God's love, God's wisdom, God's power; to the beauty of the oneness of all life.

'Let us now meditate together on the at-one-ment of life. In your meditation try to realize that you are not separate, but that you are all of the one spirit. You have to learn that humanity is one vast brotherhood of life; that all nature is part of you—you are part of nature; you are part of the animal kingdom; you are part of the air and the birds in the air and the fish in the sea; you are part of the whole of creation, because you are a part of God and all creation is God. To reach this realization you must rise in your imagination into the golden light, the supreme light, and there prostrate yourselves humbly before the Almighty God in Whom we all live and breathe; Who is Infinity and Eternity....

'This is the ancient wisdom. Life is good, so live life to the full; live to glorify your Creator. And in thankfulness for the gift of life, give from your own soul life-giving, healing rays for the blessing of all your brethren.'

6

A HEALTHY WAY OF LIFE

An important part of the Indian creed was reverence for the physical body. The people knew that the physical body is the temple of the soul; it is the channel through which the divine Spirit can manifest and the means by which the soul can learn life's lessons and do God's work. They knew that if they were to fulfil the plan of the Great Spirit for their earthly lives, then they must treat their bodies wisely. They were taught from childhood to be moderate in all things and to shun all forms of physical indulgence, and strove always through strict physical and mental discipline to keep their bodies in a state of perfect fitness and cleanliness.

White Eagle also tells us:

'It behoves all of us, when we realize the truth that the body is indeed the temple of the spirit, to keep our bodies unsullied; to treat them with the same courtesy and gentleness with which God regards them.

'Remember, my sons and daughters, that your body is the temple of God and should be used with thankfulness to glorify God. Your body is the instrument for God's work; through your body comes the power to create bodies for incoming egos. What a sacred work is yours! God will use the gifts which you give Him–Her to glorify the earth. Through your physical body, you will be able to work in partnership with God. According to your purity and love of God you will be enabled to attract, to the physical body which you can create, those highly-evolved souls who are waiting to come into incarnation, to be born into pure bodies that will give them every opportunity in the great work of bringing brotherhood upon earth.

'Keep your body pure and healthy; do not allow it to be over-strained; eat wisely, of pure food; and each day open yourself to the blessing of the Christ-spirit, that your body may be illumined by the Son of God. So will you meet one another with a blessing radiating from your heart; your hands will possess the power to heal, your words to comfort those in trouble; and your very aura will show forth the radiance of the Christ-spirit, so that every soul you encounter may feel better for having come into touch with you.

Ancient wisdom reveals that the purpose of life on earth is for every human being to become as perfect a channel or instrument as it is possible to be for the manifestation of the Christ-spirit in physical matter. The Indians knew this goal, and set their feet upon the path to its attainment. How far they would have progressed without interference from the white civilization we cannot guess, but it seems to me that our so-called civilization has much to learn from their example.

Indian children came to love and worship the Great Spirit,

to love all beings, to love all creatures of the earth and their Mother Earth herself. Ohiyesa, the celebrated Indian writer quoted in TOUCH THE EARTH, says: 'As a child I understood how to give; I have forgotten this grace since I became civilized. I lived the natural life, whereas I now live the artificial. Any pretty pebble was valuable to me then; every growing tree an object of reverence. Now I worship with the white man before a painted landscape, whose value is estimated in dollars!'

Again and again White Eagle's teaching shows evidence of his life among these ancient American Indians; and that his mission with us is to bring back their pure and vital way of life into a sick world. For instance, he tells us:

'While you live on the earth you are building a temple. First of all you are building your physical body by your daily habits, by the food you eat and the air you breathe. Then you are building your astral body by your desires and emotions; you are building your mental bodies—the lower mental body—by your habitual daily thought, and the higher mental by the imagination of your creative self. All these bodies are visible in the aura. In order to contact the higher realms of life, you must develop senses with which to do it; your subtler bodies must be pure and light in order that you may contact these pure and subtle planes of life. If you are content to grovel with crude material things, your subtler bodies will be coarse and you will remain imprisoned in an earthly condition. You seek to perfect the physical body by right living, right aspiration and true prayer; to purify the astral body by heavenly desires, by spiritual aspiration and refined tastes; the mental body by meditation and creative imagination. All the time you are reaching up you are building your subtler bodies of a fine and pure substance. Until you have these bodies, you are living in a kind of prison house.

'All that the soul ever does and experiences on the earth is built into its temple of light in the heaven world. When you build a house you have to make the plans; you have to engage your workers and gather your materials. When all is ready you begin to build. So it is in the spirit world: there is this slow gathering together of the material to build your temple or home of light. The home of light in the spirit world is the celestial body, but neither this nor any of the bodies can be made beautiful if the physical life is not lived in harmony with God's law.'

Because the Indians were taught that the body is the sacred temple of the spirit, they did their utmost to retain it in the peak condition of youth. Their physical fitness and prowess, I believe, surpassed that of any other race—possibly because no other race lived as close to nature and the natural way of life intended by the Great Spirit when He–She created the human body.

White Eagle tells us that the Indians' pure way of life enabled them to become not only physically, but also emotionally and nervously, stronger than we are.

He says:

'You have asked whether the Indian was emotionally tougher and less sensitive than people are today, and if it was easier for them than it is for the white race, which you say is more sensitive. I think it is true to say that the Indian had developed certain qualities of detachment: in other words, the Indians did not allow their emotions to overcome them. They had developed a simple and pure spirituality which meant that they were not dominated by their nervous system, as is the white man who lives a more artificial life. The Indian lived close to nature and obeyed natural laws. Men and women of today are softer than the ancient Indian, because their lives are more artificial, and over-development of the intellect makes them weaker nervously than was our robust Indian brother or sister. The Indian was strong nervously as well as physically, and so was better able to withstand emotional strain and the buffetings which overcome white men and women. In a certain way they were more developed, more receptive to unseen influences, owing to their close contact with nature. Life develops on a spiral and, as every man or woman goes through his or her various stages of evolution, in one life he or she develops one soul-aspect, and in another he or she develops a second aspect. The complete being is like a jewel with many facets, and each facet is a quality of character and a quality of life.'

We know that the Indian of recent times combined physical prowess with bravery of a quite exceptional and outstanding quality. In the terrible and cruel war which modern white people have waged against the Indians, it was well known among the white soldiers that one white soldier was no match for one Indian. From the very ancient days the Indians were taught that perfect health of the physical vehicle could only be retained by a threefold path—pure living at the physical level, pure thoughts and pure actions—that is to say, always acting in harmony with the law of the Great Spirit.

White Eagle says:

'Every pupil who entered the mystery school of the Brotherhood began his or her studies by disciplining and purifying the physical body. He or she learnt to eat pure food and never to inflict suffering upon the animal kingdom. He or she learnt of the vitality and life in the air, and how consciously to breathe in the life-forces of the air. He or she learnt the cleansing property of the element water, not only for the physical body, but also for the psyche; and therefore the neophyte* made a ritual of his daily ablution.

'He or she learnt how to draw strength from the earth, and how consciously to absorb into the body the life-giving rays of the Sun. In other words, he or she was taught to become purified, revivified and sustained by simple attunement to the elements.

'As people learnt to use all those elements in their

*I.e., the student, the one training for initiation in the mystery school.

daily lives, their physical bodies became purer, lighter, less weighed down with the earth, thus enabling the spirit to come into fuller contact, through the physical body, with other beings, with the whole great brotherhood of life.'

In the ancient days, as we have already seen, the brothers and sisters taught that human beings should live in brotherhood with all forms of life. How can one equate such a need for brotherhood between all the kingdoms with killing—especially with killing for food, as the American Indian must have done?

White Eagle says:

'When a soul has evolved to a degree of adeptship, when it understands the divine law of sowing and reaping, it knows that it cannot violate Mother Earth without hurting itself; that it cannot slay another in war without suffering a similar fate someday; that it cannot slay and eat the animals and, still worse, hunt the poor creatures for sport, without itself enduring exactly the same degree of suffering that has been inflicted on the lesser creatures. It is not necessary for humanity to consume flesh for its bodily wellbeing. In the very early days before Indian culture degenerated they lived harmlessly and in brotherhood with all life.

'They never killed animals for fun, nor yet for sport; they only killed for food when it was absolutely necessary for survival. When they had to do so they thanked brother animal for the food its body was supplying. In other words, the law of love prevailed throughout all

American Indian life. The Indians were good people, a fine and noble race and nearer to the Great Spirit in their hearts than many of the educated and sophisticated white people who sometimes enjoy killing for fun, which is a very different matter. It is not necessary for you, living as you do in the temperate zone, to kill at all—and we advise you to live on the fruits, and grains of the earth, which are the natural food of human kind.

'The true brother–sister of earth seeks to live healthily, which means in holiness and purity. Such a one seeks to live harmlessly and joyously, lives to radiate the light and beauty and the love and truth of God, and loves all creatures. Such a being could not wantonly inflict pain. All life is one, and all life is governed by the divine law of love. Each person will have to suffer every hurt, every cruelty inflicted upon any form of life because actually he–she has inflicted it upon him- or herself. Once you recognize that you are part of an infinite, universal life, you will know that you cannot hurt anything—any part of God's creation—without injuring yourselves; because you are part of everything that lives, and everything that lives is part of yourselves.

'The food you eat supplies nourishment to the different types of atoms in your physical and etheric bodies; so if you eat coarse food, you are stimulating and feeding the coarser atoms. Likewise, if you naturally have a taste for sun-nourished food—sun-kissed fruit, ripened corn and mountain water, and the berries and the nuts of the trees—you are feeding the higher, the aspiring atoms in your being, you are assisting your spiritual training. If you insist upon the coarser types of food, it makes your training harder and longer.

'You know, the brothers of old always used water, perhaps more than once a day they bathed the whole physical body in water. They drank water. They used water extensively in healing. We suggest that a bowl of water, and a pretty bowl—a lovely colour, perhaps the colour of amethyst or the colour of rose—should be filled and refilled with clear water frequently and left in the sun, so that the rays of the sun can impregnate that water with life-force, with the healing ray. And then that water could be taken by the mouth, just a little, not the whole bowlful.'

Reverence for life, for the Great Spirit and for Mother Earth, also gave the Indian a reverence and love for all the gifts of Mother Earth: fresh fruit and grains, pure crystal water from the mountain streams, all that was pure and wholesome and whole. This helped to make his bodies strong and healthy. How different from us today!—with our much-refined and adulterated flour, the artificial flavourings, preservatives, sweetness and all the thousand-and-one chemicals and processes used in so much of our food. But even now we can see the beginning of a revolt against these things, and a return to the pure and natural way of life; and modern culture is learning at last that you pollute and desecrates Mother Earth and her gifts at your own peril.

White Eagle tells us:

'Now when humanity is able to comprehend the vast-ness of the universe; when people are able to call down and command the sunlight, the great white light which the Great Spirit is offering to human kind, down on to their crops: then there will be no need for the poisons which you are using today. We cannot advocate too strongly the wisdom of natural growth, natural heal-ing, natural spiritual expression of the love of the Christ within the human heart. All these truths which are embodied within Divine Law should be learnt and applied by human kind.'

The Indians were also taught that almost as important for physical health as the quality of the food they ate was the air they breathed. I have described how they were taught to go out each morning into the fresh air and stand before the rising sun, breathing deeply and absorbing into their very being the healing and strengthening rays of the Sun. One can imagine what it must have been like to rise each morning and stand gazing over the valleys and tall trees to the sunlit mountains beyond, breathing deeply of the pure air. All the problems of physical life would fall away, as one became attuned to the harmony and order of nature and of all life. One would breathe in the sunlight of God, and breathe out and away the cares of physical life.

White Eagle tells us:

'One of the finest methods of which we knew in our

American Indian days for the strengthening of the finer bodies and nervous system was by deep breathing. People little realize the importance of breathing correctly, and how the art of breathing can be used to cleanse and revivify not only the physical body but every part of your being.

'We suggest this simple exercise. On rising, face the Sun, if possible before an open window (which should have been open all night). Stand erect so that you are correctly polarised, with the spine straight, the solar plexus controlled, heels together, toes slightly apart. Before you inhale, centre your whole concentration upon the light, upon the Sun. As you become enfolded by and absorb the golden rays of the Sun, the Great Spirit, Father–Mother God, you will feel in your heart a sense of loving dependence upon the Father–Mother. Try to realize your relationship with the Great Spirit. Now take your breath; and as you breathe, realize that you are breathing not only air but very life-atoms into your being. Raise your arms as you breathe in, if you find it helpful; and then as you breathe out let your arms fall slowly. You breathe in and absorb this stream of life and light from the Father–Mother God, and then you let it fall from you in blessing upon others. So you absorb God's life, and you bless all life. You receive and you give; and so you come into harmony with the rhythmic lifestream. It will feed your nerves, and give you a sense of peace and control.

'After doing this exercise for two or three days, don't

then say, "I am too late today, I can't do it." You must discipline yourself until your daily communion becomes so natural that you would not miss it. It will become an automatic action, and so you will become *en rapport* with the universal life-force, as were your brothers and sisters among the Indian in those days of long ago.

'The Indian never hurried this morning communion with the Great Spirit and the angels of the elements. It was an essential part of his or her life and one which never failed to bring renewed vitality and strength of purpose for the day's tasks which lay ahead. Deep breathing brings an inner tranquillity, a steadiness and valuable help in facing any ordeals which lie ahead. A master never allows him- or herself to become flustered or worried; a master can face anything with perfect calm.

'In this way the ancients were taught how to draw to themselves through their thought and feelings the rays of life-force essential to physical health. They would call upon the air and the air spirits would come to them, and they would be able to see the sylphs and the spirits of the air. They knew how to open their hearts in simplicity to the Great Sun, to worship that Sun, and receive a concentration of the Sun's rays into their hearts; and the light and the warmth of the Sun's rays would pass all through their bodies causing them to tingle with health. They understood what they were doing; that is to say they used their minds to concentrate and direct the rays. At the same time, the feelings of their etheric body were stimulated, so that through this they were able to *feel* the invisible power of the Sun; they were able to feel too the invisible power of the air, the invisible power of the water, and of the very earth itself. Why, we remember in our time (and many of you were with us then), we children used to have a game when we would stand erect with our backs against the trunk of the tree calling upon the spirit of the tree to give us strength; and we would feel the life-force of the tree coming into our physical body, into the spine and through the limbs. So much has been lost by the people of the present day!

'Our brothers and sisters among the Indians were perfect physically, and spiritually much in advance of so many people in the sophisticated societies of today. Have you ever watched a Native American walking? You should take a lesson from that. Think for a moment of the difference in your attitude of mind immediately you pull yourself erect and aspire. You seem to be filled with light, and this is exactly what happens when you stand erect, perfectly poised. The spiritual light is able to enter and pass through you without hindrance, to your fingertips and down your spine to its base; and your feet (free and supple, as they should be) are able to feel and draw magnetism from the earth, and this magnetism circulates through your aura, giving you that vitality and energy for which you long.

'It is most important to keep the spine lifted so that the energy of the Sun spirit can pour through the head and descend down the spine. The body elemental is attached to the lower forms of life, it wants to slouch, but the ego wants to stand upright. An erect spine helps to keep the soul in touch with the higher self, rather than to remain under the influence of the body elemental. You can get a straight back as much from the mind as the body.'*

A great deal of ill-health nowadays is caused simply by the pressure of life and the consequent state of tension which comes from anxiety of body and mind. In the far-off days of which I am speaking, the Indian was quite free from the pressures of commercialism and the over-stimulation of the mind and desires from which we today suffer. The Indian was not driven by manmade time-values but lived in rhythm with the changing seasons and the rising and setting of the Sun. He or she was able to live at a much gentler, calmer pace, relaxed and at peace with the world—a tranquillity which we should do well to emulate if we would find perfect health.

White Eagle tells us:

'So few earthly people know how to relax. I see tense sleeping bodies, faces screwed up, instead of a beautiful relaxation, peace, and surrender to the heavenly spheres. When you go to bed at night, let your body rest at ease, your mind be calm and still, and let the celestial body fill the aura with the light of Christ, in this way you will prepare yourself to go forth from your

*Note that the spine has a natural curve to it and so to have a lifted spine is not to have a puffed-out chest!

body into higher worlds; here you will undergo spiritual experiences which will so impress the mind that you will wake in the morning with a gentle memory of something wonderful having happened. In this preparation for sleep—and the way you sleep—you are training yourselves to receive divine illumination, and freedom from the chains of bondage of earthly life.'

From the moment of waking until the moment of sleep, the Indian of these far-off days endeavoured to live as healthy and as natural a life as possible and in a spirit of brotherhood with all other creatures. This spirit of brotherhood included his or her thoughts as well, for the Indian knew that thoughts have a profound effect on physical life and wellbeing.

White Eagle tells us:

'It is not only the food that you eat that matters, but your thoughts and your general outlook on life. Remember that your bodies—physical, mental, astral and spiritual—are the temple of the holy Spirit, of the God within. Therefore you must attune yourselves to all good: the good vibration, the aspiring vibration. Your whole life is lived within a concentration of cosmic forces, and as a magnet you draw to yourselves conditions and powers like those you have awakened in yourselves. What you think, you become; the vibrations you set in motion by your thoughts make an impression on the ether, and attract to you corresponding waves or forces, which create certain conditions in your physical body and life. Begin your work for the Brotherhood through your daily good thought. Think good—*be* good. Think love—*become* love. If you think harmony, you become harmony. Your progress begins with your own thought. Thoughts take form. See that your thought-forms are created of goodness and beauty. God created all things by thought. You can remake your bodies, your lives, your happiness, your health by the power of thought—your own thought.

'The brothers of the Cross of Light did indeed teach the ancient Indians to turn their thoughts to God on every possible occasion, and to see God, or good, in everything that happened and every aspect of their lives. This did not mean living with their heads in the clouds, but rather seeing God's hand, God's love everywhere, and in all circumstances. The Indians always looked for the positive, the happy, the hopeful aspect of whatever happened; because they always thought in this way they were happy and at peace.'

'You have never heard us telling you to put on sackcloth and ashes. God has placed you in this world to give you joy and happiness. God has placed you in a beautiful world. God has given you a beautiful body and He–She has placed in your heart the key to enter the place of all happiness. Enjoy your life. Be happy and thankful for every glorious sensation which your body rightly gives to you. Enjoy your food. Let it be clean, pure food. Enjoy your recreation. Enjoy all forms of bodily exercise. Enjoy every good gift of life, but never forget the Source of your life to which you owe everything. That is the secret, that is the way.

'Live in spirit. Live by the spirit and let your heart love much. Love life. Love everything. Love all peoples, but above all love the Perfect One, the Christ in the heavens; and love your Creator, your Father–Mother God. Give thanks for your creation and live to glorify your Father–Mother in heaven.

'When you can live in complete harmony and brotherhood with all life, you will retain perfect health of the physical vehicle throughout the earthly life.'

7

NATURAL HEALING

White Eagle tells us that in the very early days of which he speaks, the art of healing by spiritual and natural or nature methods was highly developed. In any civilization, however perfect, there are the younger ones who cannot live up to the high standards of disciplined living necessary if the body is to retain perfect health and vitality. Moreover, some disease is karmic in origin; that is to say, the soul has voluntarily accepted it before reincarnating, in order to learn certain lessons.

And so a system of healing was developed and taught in the mystery schools and temples of the past. Tests of both physical and spiritual self-discipline and endurance had to be undergone before the candidate was accepted for training. The training itself was rigorous because as well as a knowledge of anatomy and herbal remedies, much spiritual understanding was also necessary. Knowledge also of music was required: of the power of sound; for in the ancient days, rays of colour linked with perfume and sound were used to heal the body and the soul. There is no lasting bodily healing unless the originating soul disturbance is healed. The healer had to preserve his or her body in health too, so that it became a pure and perfect channel for the healing rays of the Christ Light (by

Christ we mean not the man Jesus, but the Light, the Sun, the great Spirit common to all religions and all races).

The dis-eased were also treated by herbs and natural remedies, and by a combination of colour, sound and perfume. These ancient peoples were masters of their crafts, and in the temple they were able to obtain pure and living rays of colour by shining white light through exquisitely cut and polished jewels. The physical presence of the colour, used in conjunction with the colours which were mentally projected by the healers and carried to the patients by the healing angels, produced wonderful results and 'miracles' of healing.

White Eagle has been asked why many of the healing helpers and guides who come back from the world of spirit to help people on earth today are American Indians, or perhaps those who learnt about the white magic in Polynesia or the Maori race? He tells us:

'The American Indians retain knowledge of medicine handed down from a remote antiquity, from the healing schools of the lost continents of Mu and Atlantis, for these ancient races were well instructed in the art of true healing. They were taught the inner secrets of the natural healing forces; of the healing magic, the Sun's rays, and the herbs of the earth. They knew about the healing properties of herbs and flowers and the leaves and bark of the trees and how to use these remedies which nature has provided for the cure of all disease. They were conversant with the "little people" and the guardians of the law of God. They were conversant with both natural and spiritual law, and were taught by the priests of the white magic how to commune with healing angels. They knew that every flower and plant that grows has its own vibration of God, and that every flower has an affinity with some part of the human organism. They knew that not only the physical substance of the flower but also its colour and planetary vibration have an effect on some centre in the human organism, for plants as well as humans come under the influence of the planets. It is truly said that there is a herb for the cure of every disease. When humanity today is able to understand and use the simple natural remedies, the physical body will soon be restored to its natural equilibrium.

'When the physical body needs soothing, comforting and healing, always turn to Mother Nature. In nature you have everything you need for the healing of the ills of the body. In the new age, all healers, all doctors, will come to recognize that the natural way of healing is by herbs, by prayer, by colour rays, by perfume and sounds (for all these are linked) and by sacramental methods such as spiritual healing. By all these simple natural ways will the healing of the body be accomplished in the new age, as it was in the ancient civilizations of America.

'We remember—and you too may remember, for some of you were with us then—how in those days we received instructions from the Plumed Serpents. They were the priests and priestesses of the Indian mystery schools—school, we had better say. Those Indians who had attained a degree of knowledge and spiritual understanding were called the Plumed Serpents of the people. We learned from them the art of healing by touch, by manipulation, by the juices of herbs and flowers, and by the reception into our consciousness of the great white light: all these things were taught in our Sun temples. For in those days the healer was a teacher as well as a healer; when the healer visited the people they were touched in their hearts by the nobility and purity of the healer's physical presence, as well as by the light which poured from his or her soul.

'The wise teacher first taught us pupils to attune ourselves to the first great Cause, to become in harmony with the light (the Sun); and to develop that continual attitude of mind which could neither think ill of nor do harm to any living thing. Thus the pupil made him- or herself a pure channel for the light.

'Spiritual healing is based on spiritual science, and the source of all healing of the physical body is the Sun. Call it light, call it love, it all means the same thing: that one true source of all life. Light, which is love, is the great healer.

'There must also be perfect peace and tranquillity in the soul of the would-be healer. There must be an inflow into the instrument of divine energy. Love is the creator of divine energy, and the healer must draw to him- or herself, and give forth, harmony … peace … tranquillity. Such a healer is working with the white magic or the white light, and is continually sending forth healing through all his or her life.

'The priest–healer in those days was able to look into the soul of the sufferer and see not only the physical symptoms but much deeper, into the past karma of the patient; the healer would see perhaps violent emotions, hates, prejudices or intemperance, and would know how to heal the soul of these deep inharmonies, or how to help the soul to heal itself.

'The foundation of all healing is attunement by the healer to the forces of spirit and of nature. These powers are manifold and it is no easy task to take each of these threads and weave them into a grand pattern of true and perfect healing. Harmony is essential—harmony of spirit, tranquillity of spirit. The basis of ill-health is inharmony in the sufferer's soul—perhaps arising from inharmony in his or her physical conditions of life. Anything inharmonious to the individual is liable to bring certain physical symptoms. The more evolved the soul, the more attuned it becomes to the higher worlds and the spiritual life, the more acutely will inharmony be felt, and if not dealt with immediately by meditation and deep breathing and other means of restoring harmony, it will manifest later as bodily ill-health.

'Disease as it is at the present time is the result of ignorance and wrong living: the breaking of all the laws of God. This occurs not only in feeding but in the very treatment of life itself, which is polluted; the treatment of the earth, of the water, which is polluted; of the air, which is polluted. Even human thoughts are polluted. This is why we come back from the spirit life to bring a little knowledge and urge you to listen. Try out our suggestions about right thought. Right thought is God thought, good thought, goodwill; which brings right action towards all life and in regard to your own bodies. It brings control of the nervous system; correct breathing; quiet, steady living. Can you see an old chief of our nation getting in a panic and rushing about?

'If you want good health, you must endeavour to live your life in harmony with the divine law of love. This means that you do no harm, cause no suffering to any living creature. Seek for harmony in your human relationships, love all creatures; love, and your whole body will be recreated. Love Mother Earth and all her creation. Aspire to purity—pure thinking, pure living, pure food, absorbing the essence of the elements and remembering that the creative power of God is working through all these elements—earth, air, fire and water. Put yourself in tune with all nature.

'When you take a walk in the country, breathe in the air and think of the angels of the air element, and the spirits of the air. Remember that they are all about you, they are the very life in the air and they will help you and revivify you. Breathe deeply, thinking of those angels of the air and the air spirits who are with you to purify and heal you, and bring you life and refreshment.

'And again, think of the angels of fire, the angels of the Sun. If you have developed your inner vision or your power of clear sight, you will see in the dancing sunlight these angels of fire, friendly, warming, healing. But always remember that the angels of fire expect love in your heart. Love is the vehicle—shall we say?—of these angels of the fire element.

'And then think of the little elementals of the flowers, of the earth—the little servers of the great Mother Nature. In your meditations, when you close your eyes and use your power of imagination, you can see these delightful little nature spirits working under the direction of the great angels, who in their turn work within the power of the great Mother of all the earth.

'You live and work surrounded by these wonderful beings, but many of you are so blind you seldom see. You are so deaf, you never hear the song of the angels, the joy and happiness of the angels. You do not smell the perfume of the angels of Mother Earth. Seldom will you inhale the perfume of the air, the water, the Sun or the earth. Train yourself to become aware of and friendly with the nature spirits, friendly with the angels of the four elements because, if you work with them, it will increase your power to heal.

'Do what you can also to spread the message to the peoples on earth to live purely on the fruits and grains of the earth, to drink the pure waters of the earth, to breathe the pure fresh air of the earth, and to be kind and gentle with Mother Earth; to feed her with the right food, and to feed the physical body (which is part of Mother Earth) with the pure food of Mother Earth. This is all part of healing: healing for the body, healing for the soul. Your mission as a healer is to radiate quietly the healing rays put through you by the angels under the command of the heavenly Father and divine Mother, striving to become a pure and perfect channel for the light and healing rays from the Sun of God.

'Love … *love* is the magical word.'

8

THE CELEBRATIONS OF THE SUN

'In the days of which we speak, our great and wise teachers, priests and priestesses of the Sun, led their people in ceremonies and rituals through which their love and worship of the Great Spirit of all creation found reverent and rapturous expression. Through their rituals they would invoke the help and blessing of the angels and of invisible powers. The invisible rays thus invoked would stimulate their subtler, finer bodies to become receptive to the outpouring of light and blessing which came upon the earth at special seasons, such as at the solstices and equinoxes. These four festivals have been celebrated throughout the ages. Hence the stirring of the human spirit at Christmas time, the joy and thankfulness for the coming of spring; and then—when the Sun is at its zenith, the summer solstice—again there comes a stimulation of the spirit and you are filled with joy because of the colourful profusion of flowers, and the ripening fruits of the earth. This leads to the autumn equinox, the gathering-in of the harvest, which again gives cause for deep gratitude. In spite of the materialism of today, humanity still responds to these occasions, and always will do so, for such festivals are as old as the world itself.

'Although many of the present-day Christian festivals have their origin in these ceremonies of long ago, much of their spiritual power and significance has been lost, for the masses do not understand the inner meaning and the help and blessing available to them through a proper understanding and performance of ritual and ceremonies. Perhaps this explains the feeling of deadness and coldness in some churches; but when the officiant is spiritually awakened and can teach his or her flock the inner meaning of the ceremonies, then the true spiritual power will flow through the officiant and he or she will bring the light of heaven to them.

'We would help you all to understand and appreciate the invisible activity behind rituals used in religious practices. We are not suggesting that you have to go back to outworn ceremonies from which the spirit has fled, but that you should realize the power available to you through ceremony and ritual in your religious life, and even in daily life, outside your temple of worship. There is so much for you to learn concerning ritual, and how it could help you truly to worship God, and to help and heal and bless human kind. Ritual and ceremonial for each new age has always been introduced at the right time into every religion throughout the ages, and used to stimulate the subtler bodies so that people come to realize the wonder of their own true being. In the past, ritual has sometimes been used before the soul was sufficiently developed to use wisely the power thus invoked. When ritual is used ruthlessly, without love and wisdom, it is destructive, and this is what has sometimes happened in past ages. But when ritual and the power of ceremony is used with pure motives, with utter selflessness, without thought or desire for self, it becomes constructive. Then this power is white magic, it is the Great White Light, the Christ light. The magic used by the Indians in those far-off days was good, white magic.

'Movement, speech and music are all concerned in ritual. Speech correctly used can gather up invisible forces and build them into form which can be directed to a certain person or place on the physical plane, to bring healing or peace. Speech is the first agent for the control of occult force. Movement too was much used in the temples of the past. If you could see clairvoyantly what takes place with the movement of a dancer working from the spirit as well as from the mind, you would see most beautiful designs of light, forms of light, being built. When created with power and understanding, these forms of light built in the higher ether can gradually crystallize and be brought through into matter.

'Look back into the ages past; think for a moment of those vast temples that are a puzzle to your present-day students. They do not know how these huge stones were put into place; but we can tell you that they were built by the power of ritual, occult power. We remind you again that ritual is a means by which invisible forces are harnessed and used. These subtle mental forces are very real. If your inner vision were opened, you would see that where ritual is used there appear forms like whirls of light, almost like illumined smoke, and you would see these forces whirling round and round and forming into etheric pillars of light, sometimes of exquisite beauty. As time passes, these pillars of light become more tangible; and the etheric substance of which they are created eventually becomes a material substance, for etheric matter in time solidifies.'

White Eagle has often spoken of ceremonies and rituals he remembers from the far past, through which his people worshipped the Great Spirit, and invoked invisible powers. He has described, for instance, how at certain times they would gather to await the sunrise; how they would perambulate their temple

'…set in a level place in the midst of the mountains under the open sky and lit by myriad stars. The rays from other planets seen and unseen gently played upon this vast gathering…. All knew that they were worshipping under the direction of angels of light; as the first pale light of dawn appeared, a great hush fell upon the assembly, a profound stillness…. Then, suddenly, the Sun appeared and all the people turned to the light, worshipping, praising and thanking the Great Spirit for the coming of a new day. They knew that they were being strengthened and purified by rays from the Solar Logos itself; and could see, in the sunrise, angel beings and hosts of shining ones adding their blessing to send out the light over the peoples of the earth.'

The time of the full moon was also important:

'At the time of the full moon—the silver moon which the ancients regarded as the symbol of the higher mind or the intellect—we would perambulate the great mountain places in silent prayer: all was quiet except for the rhythmic tread of human feet. Under the silver moon we waited expectantly. Then came the breaking of the golden dawn, when the golden rays impregnated the silver.

'This is a mystical truth concerned with a development in your being for which everyone must work in their inner self. The intellect has to become stilled and ready to assimilate truth and to reach a certain level of understanding. At that level it is ready to receive the impregnation of the golden rays of the Sun or of the spirit. Thus the soul and the spirit meet, and are wedded. This is yet another symbol of the mystical marriage between soul and spirit.'

Then there were the ceremonies at the solstices. In the winter, Mother Earth lies dormant, life and light recede, the days are short, and everything in nature is at rest after cleansing, by the elements, of the autumn equinox. Then, in the depth of winter, at the winter solstice, comes the promise of the rebirth of life and of the Sun. In the Christian world, the time is celebrated as the birth of the Christ child, the saviour of human kind, but the rebirth of the Sun has been celebrated throughout the ages. The rebirth of the Sun is also a demonstration to humanity of the continuation of life, and that life comes again into full power after the rest and sleep of winter.

In the ancient days of which I am speaking, the ceremony of the lighting of the fire was enacted at the time of the winter solstice, and this was both symbolical of the birth of the light (the Christ child) within the human heart, and also of the return of the Sun after its winter journey. I have described the ceremony in THE ILLUMINED ONES (pages 47–8) and noted that it was from this ceremony that the much later ritual of the campfire of the North American Indians was derived, the circle round the fire symbolizing the enfoldment of the Great Spirit of love from which they were all born. White Eagle says, 'The birth of the Christ-spirit on earth is profoundly important to other worlds beside the earth planet'.

The ancients knew that the centre of the solar system is not only the physical Sun but the spiritual Sun behind it; they knew that the rays of light and power from the Sun and its spiritual counterpart which fall upon the earth and earth's humanity affects their spiritual as well as their physical life; and they were able to harness and use this solar force for their spiritual as well as their physical wellbeing.

White Eagle tells us:

'Well do we remember those sacred times during the year, when all the simple people of the villages in the land were drawn together to celebrate the Sun festivals. We remember, at the time of the solstices, the ceremonies of lighting the fire, of welcome to the Sun spirits, of which you know little or nothing. We remember also that wonderful and powerful ceremony in which we paced the path of the Sun, round and round in two great wheels, the positive and the negative. The lodge or temple we paced was not confined by walls and roof, but was open to the sky and stars. These ceremonies continued through nights and days.

'The ceremony of the rebirth of the light is as old as creation, as old as life itself on this earth, and the ancient brotherhood is still there, still enacting a grand cosmic ceremony year by year. Those participating in it are invisible now; there are human brethren and angelic brethren. If you were able to open your vision to the scene at Christmas time (the winter solstice) when the actual birth of the Christ child is enacted, you would see the most beautiful movement, hear the sound and rhythm of the music of the heavens, and hear the great paean of praise, hear the very creative power and Word which is being used. You would hear the chanting of the great AUM, the inbreathing and outbreathing, the invoking of the spirit to bless and bring something holy, good and pure to the earth with the rebirth of the light.'

The ceremonies at the time of the summer solstice were to invoke the power of the angels of the Sun, to worship the glory of the summer Sun, then at its zenith; and to help the people become receptive to the abundant blessing of spiritual Sunlight poured out upon them at this time.

'We speak of our own experiences in days gone by; but they have never really gone by, because what took place yesterday is today and will be tomorrow. All is the eternal now. At the time of the solstice full moon, a special festival is held in the spirit realms, a ceremony at which Christ the Sun comes among His disciples and pours a special blessing, a tremendous outpouring of love upon the earth. This outpouring of love is light and truth and beauty (which is in fact a spiritual food). This festival is as old as the earth itself but, though known to the ancients, it is recognized by comparatively few today.

The ancient Indians marked it by a special gathering on the physical plane. We ourselves have attended these festivals in a number of successive incarnations. At such festivals, the chiefs and the elders of the people met, clothed in their ceremonial dress, and the people came from long distances to meet in the temple. All work was laid aside as all were called to the temple, which stood on a vast plateau. There all our people met to worship the Source of all life, the great spiritual Being, the spiritual Sun of which the physical form was but the vehicle, the emblem. We worshipped this Source of life, for we knew that without that indestructible force we should cease to be. We knew that we were held in the embrace of this life-force, this vibration from the Sun. We became so attuned to this life of the Sun that we were absorbed into it, absorbed into one another. We were worked up into an ecstasy of joy impossible to describe; then, after certain ritual and dancing, happiness, and glorification of the Sun, we were held still within this divine Fire and we worshipped.... Every soul bowed in adoration of the Giver of life. There was a stillness, a hush and the pulsation through our bodies of the warm rays of the Sun. After the ceremony, there was great happiness again: great feasts, laughter and joy, dancing and merrymaking and marriage ceremonies.

'This ancient rite or ritual has come right through the ages from a distant past and is still held (on the inner planes) in Britain, at that holy place called Stonehenge, as well as other places. When you have reached a certain stage of development the curtain of mist will dissolve and you too will see the true glory of the rising Sun at the summer solstice.

'Do not think that you are far removed from such an experience. You are not. Day by day you are approaching this illumination for which you must prepare in mind and heart.'

As well as celebrations at the solstices, there were also the equinoxes. The ceremony of the vernal equinox was concerned with the angels of the Sun and the Earth, when the seed (the light) buried deep in earth (or matter) broke through the husk to show green shoots above the earth, and the whole land was arrayed in the glory of resurgent life. The ceremony of the vernal equinox became linked in Christian times with Easter. The story of the crucifixion of Christ is also the story of everyone: for in every man and woman the lower nature has to be crucified in order to release the spirit into higher realms, into a heavenly state of consciousness.

White Eagle tells us:

'In our Indian days we too worshipped and we looked towards our Christ. We called our saviour in those days Quetzlcoatl, and he came amongst us and he brought the same message: 'Love one another; help those who are grieved and know sorrow'.

'The story of the crucifixion of Jesus re-enacts for the Christian world an age-old truth. You are crucified in matter, in a material life, but when you suffer this bitter crucifixion you are drawing near to the resurrection of that spiritual life, that spirit which is within you. When that divine Light, that Son of God, starts to stir and rise in your consciousness, you come up against cruel people who take and crucify you; but this must always take place just before the individual is ready to rise. It does not necessarily come at the time of the death of the physical body. It comes at the time of the death of the lower nature, when the individual is struggling towards spiritual consciousness. His or her saviour is the Son of God, the Christ within. Many people today dismiss all belief in a personal saviour, saying that it is all wrong, that no-one can be saved by another, he or she can only be saved by him- or herself. Yes, we agree with that, but it is only a half-truth. You have not to depend only on your own nature; you have to realize that lying dormant within you is this eternal spirit which, when it rises in fuller consciousness in your soul, can find expression through your mind and

through your ordinary human life. This is your saviour; this is the light which saves every human being.'

Thus the ceremonies of the vernal equinox, as well as invoking the spirits of the Sun and the Earth, and celebrating the
Sun's resurrection (so marvellously demonstrated in the sheen
of new life visible everywhere on the earth) were to remind
the participants of the power of the human spirit to rise from
the darkness of materiality and the thraldom of the lower
nature. And the rituals and ceremonies were to stimulate and
strengthen the spirit so to do.

The autumn equinox was especially linked with the forces
of the air; the great angels of air were called upon, their purpose to cleanse and purify the earth after the harvest had been
gathered, and in preparation for the next sowing. At this time
many great thanksgiving ceremonies also took place, and it
was always a particularly happy occasion. The fruits of Mother
Earth were gathered in, and it was a time of thanksgiving to
the Great Mother, and the motherhood of all life. White Eagle describes also how the grain was blessed at this time:

'The purpose of this ceremony was to call down from
the Great Spirit the glowing white light to bless the
grain; for after it had been harvested, and what was
required for the immediate needs of the community
had been set apart, the golden grain for seed was blessed
and consecrated for the next sowing. Even then it was
never scattered carelessly without thought of the Creator, the Great Spirit, whose love and beneficence alone

would cause the grain to swell and grow. Indeed, the first thought of the Indian brotherhood was always of the Great Spirit, and the invisible hosts of the etheric or angelic kingdom and all the little nature-spirits who were called to service. In this manner the grain was made ready for its future sowing in a prepared and receptive soil.

'While the Indian people stood in prayer, in worship, and in thanksgiving, the teacher of the people explained the symbolism inherent in the sowing of the seed. They were taught that their thoughts and actions were like seeds, and they were shown the likely result of their own sowing, and of their own love for and faith in the Great Spirit. They were also shown how the human spirit itself is like a golden grain of wheat; and how the Father–Mother of all sent forth ministers among humanity to be sowers. For from the spirit world these sowers were sent forth to every part of the earth to bring food and life for the seed of every human spirit. The human spirit is part of God. Every individual soul contains within itself this seed of the Son of God, like a grain of golden light. Each receives this into his or her innermost being in the beginning, and from the beginning, by slow degrees, cultivates that spirit. But it takes a long, long time for seeds to develop and to bring forth ripened grain, the golden harvest.'

Another feast or festival White Eagle has described is the feast of remembrance or communion. He says:

'The feast of remembrance was celebrated in temples of the past, but not always under this name. It began with the bringing of bread and wine before the altar, both representing the gifts of Mother Earth to her human family. Through partaking of these gifts, these symbols of life, with true understanding, the people were raised in consciousness to be united with the Source, the Giver of life and all the necessities of life. As men and women took part in this feast of remembrance, recalling the Source of all bounty, they lost that arrogance which dulls so many earthly people to the things of spirit. They realized that all that they had, and all they were which was noble and beautiful, came from the same Source, the Father–Mother God, the spiritual Sun shining in the heavens. Earth, the great Mother, and God the Father produced food to feed the child, their son, which means you, my brother, and you, my sister, who are likewise son and daughter of the living God. They realized in this communion that all life was one; that all came from the same Source, and all returned eventually to God.

'In those days, souls had not descended so far into the depths of human bondage and of matter as they have today, and so they were more receptive. When men and women have finished with their dust and ashes and what we call their "mud-pies" and have risen to a higher level of spiritual attainment, then they will again be able to receive light and blessing into their beings through this Sun worship. Yes, the golden age will come again, on humanity's return up the spiral of life to God.

'The forms and ceremonies of which we have been speaking will come back in a more powerful and purified way and on an even higher vibration than before, because the earth is moving upward on the spiral of evolution, and so will receive more powerfully the blessing and help of the angelic ones and the Brotherhood of the Light. Men and women will then begin to understand their own potentialities. They will begin to understand their personal responsibility towards life and towards all people. Until this stimulation of the spirit has taken place, men and women do not think about the needs of other beings, but of self-preservation and gratification of their own desires. When, through receiving this spiritual power, men and women awaken in subtler bodies, an entirely new regime of life will come. Then they will truly worship and glorify their Father–Mother God; they will be aware of the healing power which will flow through them when needed. The human body, in the days that are to come, will be very different in texture from the body people use today, for it will lose its density and appear ethereal and shining. Men and women will be glorified as they themselves glorify and worship the Father and the Mother and the Son: God.

9

THE INDIAN'S TEMPLES
AND MYSTERY SCHOOLS

Many pyramids and monuments still remaining in Central America testify to the knowledge and skill of the civilization that produced them. In North America too there are many examples of Indian 'mounds' which were built for religious rituals, as temples and burial-places. White Eagle tells us:

'In the ancient days, we of the Brotherhood built temples on earth, places where our brethren could meet and be taught how to find God, how to worship God and how to unfold the God-life within themselves. The remnants of these temples are still to be seen on earth, though they are not as they were in the days when they were built. Our brethren of the ancient days were wise in the laws of God and knew how to operate them. They built these temples as holy places to meet and to receive knowledge and guidance.

'The temples were an outward expression of an inner spiritual wisdom. The builders were themselves initiates of the ancient wisdom, and were able to use soul-power in their building. The very form of the temple would then stimulate certain soul-qualities in the candidate and help the candidate to develop the centres of light within the temple of his or her own being. These ancient buildings were an expression of the harmonies of the universe. They were primarily temples of initiation, where the candidates working within them would absorb invisible influences helpful on the spiritual path. As the physical body is related to the universe, so these temples of stone relate to the main centres of the human being and the planetary influences which affect these centres.

'The buildings of the past had peculiar acoustic properties. The builders possessed knowledge which enabled them to create chambers which proved receptive to the sounds from the invisible worlds. Today many attempts are being made to invent instruments to receive the finer sound waves, so that messages can be received from the astral plane, and possibly from outer space. But then it was quite common knowledge, and the builders constructed these chambers so that they could hear voices from afar. There was thus a great harmony, a linking-up with every other aspect of life contained within this solar system. The buildings of the ancient Egyptians, the Greeks and Indians were all constructed to represent the grand harmonies of the spheres above, beyond and within the earth.

'Many temples of stone in America have yet to be uncovered. There is a saying that the light comes from the east. That is true, in one sense. But it was from the western hemisphere, from South America, that the priests set forth carrying with them their religion of Sun-worship—and more, the inner secrets of life in the spirit realms, and the life of spirit manifesting through matter, which they had been taught by the God-beings.

'The conception of the pyramid as an eternal symbol of God did not originate in Egypt but was taken from the West to Egypt. It is a symbol which indicates the path which every child of God has to take on its journey from its source to its end. As you understand more of spiritual science, you will be able to read the whole plan of life in the symbol of the pyramid. Men and women do not travel at random along the road of life; they move according to a definite plan. God, the Grand Geometrician, the Great Architect of the Universe, has conceived the plan; and the soul is itself the master builder. But first the soul must work on the solid block of stone, called in some schools of teaching the "rough ashlar", which is a symbol of itself. The rough ashlar has to be shaped and smoothed before fitting perfectly into the building. So an individual is shaped and perfected by life's experience till his or her soul becomes a perfect "ashlar" to be built into the universal Temple.

'The building of the pyramid is perfect, with exactitude and precision throughout, as you know. This was because the builders were working upon spiritual principles. There can be no slipshod method with divine building. There must be exactitude in everything. The builders had learnt that the spiritual laws governing their own being and human life were exact and precise. For instance, the law of karma, from which they knew there was no escape: if they had sinned against another, sooner or later they were bound to undergo that suffering which they had inflicted. They knew of the law of reincarnation: that they would come back again to earth; they knew that they had a purpose in life. They knew they must work to a certain plan; that they must, to the minutest detail, be perfect, be correct, in their dealings with every single person, as well as in the construction of their temples and homes.

'The pyramid is based on the square or the cube, signifying the human being encased in matter in the four elements; and teaching that men and women should live and act on the square with their brethren. The upper part of the pyramid, which is composed of four triangles, symbolizes the God from whom all human kind stems: the holy and blessed Three, Father, Mother and Son; Power, Wisdom and Love. All the good in the human being, the ancients knew, sprang from his or her recognition of, and endeavour to live life in accordance with, this First Principle. Therefore the family was holy.

'The builders of the pyramids were master masons on earth, master masons in the heavens above. As well as being masons or builders in the physical sense, they were masons in the truest spiritual sense. Their work was perfect—for there can be no careless work in the universal building, only perfect precision. Is this not so in your spiritual life? On the spiritual path none can get away with an unworthy piece of work.

'Stones have been discovered in America with markings and symbols which are clearly masonic, and it is true that our brethren there practised a form of freemasonry brought over to them from a lost continent. Freemasonry is not a modern institution—it stems from the original wisdom, available to both men and women, brought to earth by the God-beings. It is a very ancient mystery school. It may today have rather got away from its original purpose; but we, who have had more than one incarnation in an American Indian body, are able to explain to you that freemasonry was practised, most earnestly practised, by our people. Ancient freemasonry is the inner secret of how the builders of the past built not only the temples (of which few remain) but also the spiritual life of humanity which has been sustained ever since. It is not only the building with material stones which has been going on since the beginning of time, but a building of the power and the life-essence on earth. Ancient freemasonry is the way to build, the way to create and sustain life.

'True masonry is the ancient wisdom, and tells the story of the building of the temple of the human being from the foundation stone to the crowning dome. The foundation stone is the simple human life; then from that foundation comes the gradual building of the higher bodies—the building, step by step through many incarnations, of the temple of the soul, the temple of the white magic. When a man or woman is evolved, he or she will become as a temple of light, erected as upon a hill; and here the ceremonial magic takes place for the radiation of the power of God to stimulate and uplift the younger brethren in the valley of life.

'This ancient wisdom has been passed down from age to age through the secret schools of the inner mysteries. The basis of the work of all these mystery schools was to uncover the truth of life, the secrets of nature, the reason for being on earth, and the path each must follow on his or her return journey to God. They were formed so that those souls who were ready might follow a certain definite school of learning which would reveal to them these inner truths.

'To receive such knowledge, the soul of the student must be pure and simple; otherwise the knowledge passed on, and the unfolding powers could prove dangerous. Thus only selected pupils were admitted into the mystery schools, those who had proved themselves worthy and ready to receive the wisdom of creation.

'Great tests were put; the candidate endured physical and mental suffering to prove that he or she was strong and sufficiently wise not to abuse the secrets revealed to him or her, nor use them to harm others, but only for the good of the whole race or community.

'First the candidate was taught how to unfold the powers of the soul or the psyche; he or she was instructed in the method of quickening the sacred centres of the body.

The mysteries, the rites, were performed to test the candidate, to instruct him or her step by step on the upward path, to help him or her contact the seven planes of life.

'As candidates for freemasonry pass through outer ceremonies, and each ceremony has its effect on the subtler bodies of the candidate, so also with the mystery schools of the Americans. There were seven trials. Each trial or test applied to one of the several bodies of the human system; each test was stringent and difficult. The candidate had to face tests in his everyday human experience, and also spiritual tests of the quality of his or her love for God, devotion to the Brotherhood, strength of purpose, and motive. He or she was tested for courage, wisdom, soundness of mind and healthfulness of body. Candidates had to treat their physical bodies wisely, to eat pure food, and to control the desires and instincts of the body.

'The probationary path leading to initiation was sometimes symbolized by a subterranean passage which the candidate had to walk, a passage with many dark corners, many obstacles, many unexpected turns. These obstacles were to test the candidate's confidence in God's love. It is like the path of life: one walks the path, confused on every hand, misjudged perhaps. One is sad for recognized failures and troubled by many problems and sorrows. But if the candidate would walk the path of initiation, his or her confidence in God's love must first be tested to the uttermost limit. A candidate must know that God is good, and whatever comes leads to a greater understanding of God's love. When that thought is so firmly established that nothing can shake it, nothing cloud the vision, then the candidate will pass the test with shining eyes; he or she will pass through that particular initiation, and expansion of consciousness, or a greater understanding of God's love, will come.

'This is the whole purpose of life: that you shall surrender to God's love, acknowledging the Father–Mother as the supreme Spirit, giver of all good.'

Pupils from among our people were instructed in divine law and were given opportunities to learn about this law and see it in practice in various aspects of their life and study—in particular through studying the heavens, the stars and movement of the planets and their effect on life on earth. In time, when they are able to read the akasha (in which the history of all time is indelibly recorded) people will learn the truth of this statement. The Mayan Calendar is but one example of this form of study. White Eagle tells us:

'People of keen intellect often deny the influence of the planets on human life, but they have yet to learn, as the ancients learnt, of the great planetary rays which affect humans in incarnation, and how human life is planned and guided by angelic beings from the planets concerned with earth's evolution. When men and women understand and can work harmoniously with the planetary influences, they will absorb the lessons the planets have to teach them, through the many difficulties as well as joys which the planetary influences cause in human experience, over not one but many lives.

'The ancients studied what you today call astrology, but the astrology of those days dealt not only with human life but with the whole solar system, with the heavens. They were able, through their understanding, to control certain powers—not exactly electricity, but a psychic force or perhaps a cosmic power which could be drawn upon by occult methods. It could be used for lighting and heating purposes; it was a driving force.

'The people were taught the true significance of the heavenly bodies. In the ancient wisdom, not only was the Sun revered, but also the signs of the zodiac and the planets. The Sun-worship embraced these signs, and knowledge of them and their influence was used in many ways in the everyday life of the people.'

This knowledge was also used to teach the esoteric mysteries. In the mystery schools the pupils learnt the inner meaning of the four elements fire, earth, air and water, and the signs of the zodiac within each of these categories.

They learned how the angels of the elements are constantly at work in the inner, invisible worlds, helping people to build those subtler vehicles which interpenetrate the physical body and through which they are able to function on the different planes of being—that is, in the etheric, astral, mental and finally the celestial worlds. They learned how a person's birth horoscope could indicate the various soul-tests which had to be undergone during that particular incarnation: tests which would bring wisdom, enlightenment, and greater power to work with a particular element in service to life.

For instance, the water element is associated with the astral world and the desire bodies, and tests of the signs under this element are concerned with control of the emotions. The air element has to do with the development of the mental bodies, and the tests of these signs are concerned with the control of thought, learning how to use wisely this mighty power. The fire element has to do with the higher mental planes, and its tests are concerned with the understanding and use of the great creative force in life—the divine magic of love. The earth element is the one most closely linked with the physical life and the etheric world which interpenetrates it. The tests of this element are concerned with physical health, harmony and beauty—with the soul's ability to bring into full manifestation the plan of the Great Architect—the perfection of God's thought. Of all the tests perhaps those of the earth element are the most exacting, for they involve absolute control on all the other planes of life. The soul has to attain to that degree of mastery which enables it to transmute the physical atoms so that they do not die but are transformed into the celestial body, the perfected temple of the soul.

'Before the candidate could be admitted to a mystery school he or she had to be able to "sound the pass-word". This was more than just a spoken word. It was a soul-vibration of the absolute brotherhood of life, which he–she had to sound through all daily life and service, in all human contacts. He or she had to become attuned to the infinite love and wisdom and bring it right through into everyday life and action. The real key to all knowledge lies in attunement with the divine Spirit. Until men and women have found this key, the mysteries remain hidden.

'You too, throughout your daily life, are learning to sound the password which will admit you to the inner mysteries of life. In your shops and factories, offices and homes, even when you do the most menial task, you can be sounding the password. To learn the password means being on the alert always to express the spirit of the Son of God in all your relationships. When you can do this by action and thought, you are starting a vibration in your soul which sounds throughout all the spheres of spiritual life. It is a challenge, a command, a vibration which goes from you and which immediately attunes you to your Master—you become at one with him or her. Then there comes an ever-increasing ability to use this inner, secret magic. Understanding expands and power comes, and you can perform what earthly people call miracles.

'These things were taught in all the ancient mystery schools. They are taught today. The God-beings are coming back in greater power to help human kind to find this secret spring of life. It will depend on men and women themselves whether they will receive the knowledge the God-beings bring. Men and women can receive when they will.'

10

CONCLUSION

'We have explained how the inner wisdom was brought to the ancient Indians by those great ones, Sun-beings who came originally from more advanced planets; and how a centre of the Brotherhood of the Cross of Light within the Circle of Light was established in America. This Brotherhood did not cease working long ago, however, for all through the ages and all over the world simple people have been drawn together to live in accordance with the divine law of brotherhood; to practise in their lives the inner wisdom of the ancients, handed down to them through the secret schools of the inner mysteries which have existed in every civilization. They have always lived in harmony with one another and with God's laws, which govern the spiritual universe and their own being. They have learnt how to establish true communication and communion, not only with their own friends and teachers in the spirit state of life but with the ancient ones, sometimes with more advanced souls on other planets.

'They built their temples (remains of which can be found in remote places all over the world) for the worship of their God, and used their knowledge for the blessing of the community, as they had been taught. The spiritual power they generated by their love, service and worship, has remained to bless succeeding generations. In many parts of the world are to be found centres of light and spiritual power created by these brothers and sisters, the true "masons" or builders of ages past. When people on earth have learnt the rules or laws of brotherhood—right thinking, right speaking, right acting—they will be able to go to these places of power of which we speak, not only to receive an increased spiritual light in themselves, but to use the concentration that is there to project the light, broadcast the light for the blessing and advancement of human kind.

'The inner core of all brotherhood, whether of today or millions of years ago, has always been this light—the inner light in every man and woman, the Christ light, the Sun in every heart—giving to each the potentiality of becoming, one by one, in the fullness of time, a Sun-being.

'The grand Master of all Brotherhoods is the Christ, whose rule, in whatever embodiment he has come among the brotherhoods, has always been the same. Love and help all; heal the sick; comfort the bereaved and sorrowful; love nature, love the elements, and learn to understand and commune with the angels of the elements; learn consciously to cooperate with the myriad little workers (the spirits of the elements, by whose service the world is made beautiful and productive for humanity; they can grow in consciousness by their close association with human kind and thus human kind can serve them.

'Our Indian people called this teacher Quetzlcoatl—the Christ of the American Indian way. Quetzlçoatl was all love, gentleness, purity and understanding; he was a wonderful healer and counsellor to all his younger brethren. He showed us the way of a true brother.

'We from the Lodge above are trying once again to bring through to our beloved brethren this ancient wisdom, this knowledge of how to live happily and healthfully: how to live in harmony with the natural world and with spiritual law, and to reverence all life; and how to find the true beauty which God has given to every one of His children.

'We see in the future visitors coming to earth from more advanced planets than our own, and as in ancient times they will bring to humanity scientific and spiritual knowledge which will help human kind to live as God- or Sun-beings.

'We look forward to a golden age when brotherhood will be the natural and normal way of life throughout the whole wide earth, and humanity will be as one family in one spirit, without division of class, colour or creed; a true brotherhood of the spirit, embracing all life.'